Cambridge Elements

Elements in Law, Economics and Politics

Series Editor in Chief
Carmine Guerriero, *University of Bologna*

Series Co-Editors
Alessandro Riboni, *École Polytechnique*
Jillian Grennan, *Emory University*
Petros Sekeris, *TBS Education*

FINTECH REGULATION IN THE UNITED STATES

Past, Present, and Future

Jillian Grennan
Emory University

CAMBRIDGE UNIVERSITY PRESS

Shaftesbury Road, Cambridge CB2 8EA, United Kingdom

One Liberty Plaza, 20th Floor, New York, NY 10006, USA

477 Williamstown Road, Port Melbourne, VIC 3207, Australia

314–321, 3rd Floor, Plot 3, Splendor Forum, Jasola District Centre, New Delhi – 110025, India

103 Penang Road, #05–06/07, Visioncrest Commercial, Singapore 238467

Cambridge University Press is part of Cambridge University Press & Assessment, a department of the University of Cambridge.

We share the University's mission to contribute to society through the pursuit of education, learning and research at the highest international levels of excellence.

www.cambridge.org
Information on this title: www.cambridge.org/9781009475716

DOI: 10.1017/9781009417938

© Jillian Grennan 2026

This publication is in copyright. Subject to statutory exception and to the provisions of relevant collective licensing agreements, no reproduction of any part may take place without the written permission of Cambridge University Press & Assessment.

When citing this work, please include a reference to the DOI 10.1017/9781009417938

First published 2026

A catalogue record for this publication is available from the British Library

ISBN 978-1-009-47571-6 Hardback
ISBN 978-1-009-41794-5 Paperback
ISSN 2732-4931 (online)
ISSN 2732-4923 (print)

Additional resources for this publication at www.cambridge.org/grennan

Cambridge University Press & Assessment has no responsibility for the persistence or accuracy of URLs for external or third-party internet websites referred to in this publication and does not guarantee that any content on such websites is, or will remain, accurate or appropriate.

For EU product safety concerns, contact us at Calle de José Abascal, 56, 1°, 28003 Madrid, Spain, or email eugpsr@cambridge.org

FinTech Regulation in the United States

Past, Present, and Future

Elements in Law, Economics and Politics

DOI: 10.1017/9781009417938
First published online: January 2026

Jillian Grennan
Emory University

Author for correspondence: Jillian Grennan, jillian.grennan@emory.edu

Abstract: This Element provides an overview of FinTech branches and analyzes the associated institutional forces and economic incentives, offering new insights for optimal regulation. First, it establishes a fundamental tension between addressing existing financial inefficiencies and introducing new economic distortions. Second, it demonstrates that today's innovators have evolved from pursuing incremental change through conventional FinTech applications to AI × crypto as the fastest-growing segment. The convergence of previously siloed areas is creating an open-source infrastructure that reduces entry costs and enables more radical innovation, further amplifying change. Yet this transformation introduces legal uncertainty and risks related to liability, cybercrime, taxation, and adjudication. Through case studies across domains, the Element shows that familiar economic trade-offs persist, suggesting opportunities for boundary-spanning regulation. It offers regulatory solutions, including RegTech frameworks, compliance-incentivizing mechanisms, collaborative governance models, proactive enforcement of mischaracterizations, and alternative legal analogies for AI × crypto.

The co-editors in charge of this submission were Alessandro Riboni, Petros Sekeris and Carmine Guerriero

Keywords: FinTech, artificial intelligence, decentralized finance, blockchain, Securities and Exchange Commission

© Jillian Grennan 2026

ISBNs: 9781009475716 (HB), 9781009417945 (PB), 9781009417938 (OC)
ISSNs: 2732-4931 (online), 2732-4923 (print)

Contents

1 Introduction 1
2 The Rise of FinTech (Past) 6
3 The Economics of FinTech Growth (Present) 23
4 The Regulation of FinTech (Present) 61
5 The Path Forward in FinTech Regulation (Future) 96
6 Conclusion 110

References 113

1 Introduction

It is rare to witness the birth of a new technology, a new tool for entrepreneurship, a new investable asset class, and a new way of controlling financial decisions. Yet financial technologies (FinTech) represent all four, and so, unsurprisingly, their applications and the advancements that underlie them, like AI and blockchain, have sparked much fascination.[1] While these technologies advance rapidly, existing statutes and regulatory frameworks have not kept pace. The resulting regulatory uncertainty, exacerbated by coordination failures across agencies and jurisdictions in the United States (U.S.), risks stifling innovation and limiting benefits for consumers and small businesses. Although regulation must adapt, substantial uncertainty remains about what market failures and economic distortions may arise and what regulatory tools will mitigate them effectively.

In this study, I examine FinTech regulation through an economic and institutional lens. To analyze how regulation can effectively evolve requires understanding the economic forces driving FinTech development. I use a temporal structure (past, present, and future) to contextualize FinTech's evolution and highlight emerging regulatory trade-offs. This temporal approach is valuable for seeing the dynamics and parallels between these transformative technologies, and the synergies between their emergent combination (AI × crypto). Without comprehensively understanding the institutional and economic purposes across technologies, such as platform-building in initial coin offerings (ICOs), extending existing regulations often leads to simplistic solutions like banning ICOs because the costs associated with fraud prevention are deemed excessive. Furthermore, this high-level, temporal approach permits novel insights into what regulatory solutions can reduce economic distortions across the financial system and enable long-term stability.

I begin by characterizing the rise of FinTech and comparing and contrasting it with historical examples. Traditionally, financial innovation delivers core financial functions, such as transferring value, managing risk, and mobilizing savings, more efficiently or inclusively. However, the current wave of innovation differs from historical ones. First, the locus of innovation has shifted from incumbent financial institutions marginally improving a single product or service to technology-focused entities redesigning financial infrastructure. By creating entirely new financial infrastructures, developers combine multiple

---

[1] I recognize that the definition of FinTech itself is imprecise and discuss it in more detail in Section 2.1, where I define FinTech as any innovation meant to improve or, importantly, build upon the six core capabilities supplied by well-functioning financial systems Freixas and Rochet (2008).

types of innovation in the sense of Schumpeter (1934) that encompass new products, processes, markets, and supply, even creating new opportunities for core financial capabilities or at least blurring previous boundaries. Finally, much of this innovation is open-source and composable, unlocking tremendous entrepreneurial activity that was traditionally impossible in financial services without being a bank.

Empirical evidence from a comprehensive dataset on FinTech startups and their fundraising activity between 2012 and 2024 shows that while conventional FinTech initially dominated funding and entry, AI and crypto ventures have gained significant momentum, with the AI × Crypto domain growing especially rapidly recently. Geographic analysis shows that the U.S. and China display dense footprints across nearly all FinTech domains, with the U.S. exhibiting an exceptionally high concentration of AI × Crypto startups, suggesting an advanced position in integrating these technologies and underscoring the urgency for regulatory clarity that properly considers the parallels across FinTech domains.

Next, I examine the specific catalysts for the current wave of financial innovation, including institutional ones like the great financial crisis and technological ones like meaningful cost reductions brought about by digitization (Goldfarb and Tucker, 2019). Then, I show parallels in the economics underlying four distinct yet interrelated domains of FinTech innovation, including conventional FinTech applications (e.g., peer-to-peer lending and crowdfunding), AI-powered financial services (e.g., robo-advising and asset management), blockchain-based solutions (e.g., decentralized finance (DeFi), decentralized autonomous organizations (DAOs), non-fungible tokens (NFTs), and other Web3 applications), and finally, emergent AI × crypto services.

From an economic perspective, AI decreases the cost of prediction and exploration (Agrawal et al., 2018). AI has many use cases in finance, including robo-advisors, equity research, risk assessment, and credit scoring (D'Acunto et al., 2019; Berg et al., 2020; Cao et al., 2020; Grennan and Michaely, 2021). More recently, portfolio management, asset pricing, and even corporate finance are also areas that have benefited from the latest AI advances, such as transformer methods, reinforcement learning, and large language models (LLMs). For instance, "AlphaPortfolio" developed by Cong et al. (2021) and tree-based asset pricing methods pioneered by Cong et al. (2023a) are some examples of applications going beyond off-the-shelf to tap into the power of AI. A point of tension with AI development is that algorithms can be biased or built upon data that violates privacy concerns (Bartlett et al., 2022; Cong and Mayer, 2022). A layered regulatory approach is emerging to ensure AI systems are trustworthy and provide at least some baseline protections. For example, federal frameworks often incorporate voluntary industry standards, states reference federal guidelines when crafting local laws that may exceed federal requirements, and companies design practices to comply with and anticipate future regulations. However, more forward-looking, adaptive frameworks will be necessary as AI evolves.

Smart contracts, which are software programs potentially with AI capabilities stored on a blockchain that can receive external data in real-time and execute when certain conditions are met, enable a new category of financial service entrants called decentralized finance (DeFi) (Harvey et al., 2021; John et al., 2022). From an economic perspective, DeFi is automation that reduces market power by democratizing access to financial services, while enhancing commitment mechanisms through transparent and secure transaction records. These benefits can reduce the cost of building and/or coordinating complex financial and managerial services. Yet in reality, the distributed DeFi structures might be costly to maintain and even more challenging to coordinate. Thus, consistent with other FinTech innovations, DeFi simultaneously reduces existing economic inefficiencies while introducing new ones. Therefore, it is essential to consider these novel costs when evaluating the efficiencies gained from circumventing traditional financial intermediaries and their associated fees, inefficiencies, and potential for rent-seeking behavior.

While capital began to be meaningfully raised for AI × crypto projects around 2020, primarily in data and compute, the generative AI boom of 2022 accelerated crypto developers' interest in integrating these two technologies. Projects typically fall into four subcategories: compute, data, models, and applications. Compute projects create marketplaces leveraging idle GPU resources, offering flexible, lower-cost solutions than centralized alternatives. Data-focused ventures use blockchain-enabled marketplaces to monetize and exchange high-quality data efficiently. Model-oriented projects incentivize decentralized contributions of specialized AI models, while application-focused platforms combine frontier AI with blockchain to disseminate AI agents on blockchains. For example, some agentic applications act as decentralized autonomous entrepreneurs (DAEs) such as the Gaka-chu (Ferrer et al., 2023), thus creating a seemingly new core financial capability catalyzed by synergies at the intersection of AI and crypto.

Legal frameworks hardly exist for AI × crypto applications, especially those with a capacity for autonomous financial transactions. Therefore, I evaluate different legal analogies for their recognition, including corporate personhood, animal rights, and product liability. Corporate personhood might provide a locus of responsibility, treating AI systems similarly to corporations with defined rights and obligations. Alternatively, an analogy to animal rights could suggest basic protections against exploitation, while product liability frameworks could hold developers accountable for harmful outcomes resulting from defective AI products. Each analogy has strengths and limitations, leading me to conclude that future frameworks may need to evolve toward hybrid models that integrate aspects of these various legal analogies to maintain existing societal rights and duties.

The insights from AI × crypto integration suggest that FinTech innovations, despite their benefits, can create or exacerbate familiar economic distortions such as agency conflicts, information asymmetries, moral hazard, and coordination failures. Therefore, my analyses highlight instances where standard regulatory tools like the price mechanism and entry/exit solutions can mitigate such distortions. For example, stablecoin reserve requirements mitigate distorted economic incentives through a price mechanism, or licensing requirements can be used to screen out low-quality service providers.

At the same time, there are legal areas where applications of existing precedent are more contentious. In such instances, regulatory frameworks must adapt to these challenges. For example, the U.S. Securities and Exchange Commission (SEC) applied logic from a prior case in what has become known as the "Howey Test" to clarify when a token transitions from a "security" to a "utility token."[2] The determining factors are the expectation of profit and the extent of decentralization. Unsurprisingly, developers of DeFi applications make subtle design choices so that an expectation of profit is not present. These design choices enable developers to fail the Howey Test and thereby avoid the burden of compliance with securities regulation. Or as an AI example, in 1939, Supreme Court Justice Felix Frankfurter coined the phrase "fruit of the poisonous tree" in developing doctrine governing the admissibility of evidence in court (Frankfurter, 1939). As the metaphor suggests, if the "tree," or a source of evidence, is tainted, so is its "fruit." A parallel concept for the importance of data integrity in AI-driven financial products has recently been applied, suggesting that illegitimately acquired data may taint the entire AI-based model or application.

Another frequently disputed topic is secondary liability, which could create issues for DeFi aggregators, liquidity providers, and even DAO community members if the DAO facilitates unlawful behavior. While safe harbors may provide a solution for well-intentioned DeFi creators, it is worth noting that

---

[2] The legal distinction may not match the designer's intent (Cong and Xiao, 2021; Lambert et al., 2021). In fact, there are many more token categorizations based on design, including payment, platform, product, and cash-flow-based tokens.

perpetual safe harbors, such as those associated with Section 230 for platform companies, appear to have long outlived their use (Citron and Wittes, 2017; Smith and Alstyne, 2021). Notably, at their discretion, most platform companies adjudicate disputes (e.g., over copyright infringement, appropriateness of content, and/or counterfeit products). Despite several attempts, no private solution for a blockchain-based adjudication system has gained much traction. From a forward-looking perspective, RegTech-enabled adjudication could be a promising area for regulators to step in.

Next, I explore modifying existing regulatory tools, such as offering safe harbors with sunset provisions, and new regulatory applications such as RegTech, a term encompassing FinTech innovations that enhance the regulatory process. For example, many traditional market manipulation tactics, including wash trading and pump-and-dump schemes, port to digital asset markets. These practices undermine market integrity, inflate project valuations misleadingly, and harm investor trust. Regulators have intensified efforts to curb such manipulative practices through enforcement actions. Enhanced surveillance and transparency (e.g., RegTech-embedded monitoring and even automated enforcement) could deter market manipulation further. RegTech can also help with the complexities of finding solutions for jurisdictional issues, such as taxation, and compliance issues (e.g., portable Know Your Customer (KYC)). This is critical as many cybercrimes have been enabled by DeFi capabilities (Cong et al., 2023c), yet we also know that blockchain transparency and forensics can help regulators to detect and prosecute criminals (Cong et al., 2023b).

While adapted regulatory tools and RegTech solutions are promising, the sheer magnitude of new risks emerging from rebuilding the infrastructure for financial services means regulators will need a multifaceted approach. Thus, encouraging aspects of self-regulation with governmental oversight, such as adopting standardized approaches and metrics for decentralization, would be beneficial as would be collaborative governance arrangements, such as regulatory sandboxes, where stakeholders, including developers, incumbents, academics, and consumer advocates, must overcome adversarial positions and engage with regulators to create balanced policies. Importantly, though, in doing so, the collaborators must credibly commit to not tilting the rules in favor of a single participant in the sandbox.

The remainder of the Element is structured as follows: Section 2 establishes the historical context of financial innovation, defines core financial functions, and presents data documenting the rise of FinTech startups. Section 3 examines the economic incentives shaping innovation and market entry across specific

FinTech domains and common distortionary forces. Section 4 reviews existing regulatory approaches, and Section 5 proposes actionable regulatory solutions before concluding.

2 The Rise of FinTech (Past)

2.1 Defining FinTech through Core Financial Functions

FinTech has become a catch-all term for innovations that leverage digital tools to deliver financial services more efficiently, inclusively, and transparently. In a seminal paper, Philippon (2016) defines FinTech as covering

> digital innovations and technology-enabled business model innovations in the financial sector. Such innovations can disrupt existing industry structures and blur industry boundaries, facilitate strategic disintermediation, revolutionize how existing firms create and deliver products and services, provide new gateways for entrepreneurship, democratize access to financial services, but also create significant privacy, regulatory, and law enforcement challenges. Examples of innovations that are central to FinTech today include cryptocurrencies and blockchain, new digital advisory and trading systems, artificial intelligence and machine learning, peer-to-peer lending, equity crowdfunding and mobile payment systems.

While this definition is prescient and informative, to understand the institutional context in which FinTech emerged, one must lay the groundwork by answering foundational questions from the past. First, what core functions does the financial system provide, and why are these functions central to economic activity? Second, what allocative or productive inefficiencies justify governments and regulators intervening in the supply and demand dynamics of financial services?

Economic theory identifies six core capabilities supplied by well-functioning financial systems, for example, see detailed explanations in Freixas and Rochet (2008). First, financial markets enable the clearing and settling of payments to facilitate commerce. From ancient barter systems to modern online payments, finance ensures that buyers and sellers can transact with confidence, minimizing counterparty risk (i.e., the probability that one party in a financial transaction will default on their contractual obligation, resulting in a loss for the other party) and transaction costs (i.e., all expenses incurred in the process of exchange beyond the price of the good or service itself such as search costs, bargaining costs, and enforcement costs associated with contract fulfillment).

Second, financial markets provide mechanisms for pooling funds to undertake large-scale projects. This pooling function makes it possible to assemble capital from diverse sources, ranging from individual savers to corporate treasuries to institutional investors. This pooled capital can then be channeled into ventures too large or complex for any single entity. Moreover, by subdividing ownership (i.e., through securitization processes such as those associated with issuing equity), financiers allow investors to diversify across multiple businesses, thus managing their exposure to risk from any single default or loss.

A third function of the financial system, particularly that of intermediaries, is transforming assets to facilitate better resource transfer across time or maturity, region or denomination, and industries. Finance allows households to save today for future consumption (e.g., via retirement savings), permits firms to invest capital in high-return projects (e.g., via corporate venture capital), and facilitates reallocating tangible and intangible assets when economic conditions shift. This intermediation balances the liquidity needs of firms and households while fostering a more dynamic economy. A fundamental feature of this resource transfer and reallocation is that the underlying assets have been transformed to better meet the demands of various actors.

Fourth, and related to the transformation of assets, is the transformation of risk-return profiles and the ability to manage risk. Financial instruments and markets offer many ways to manage risk. Through insurance contracts, derivatives, or loan syndication, parties can price, hedge, and distribute different types of risk. This bundling and decomposition of risk-and-return profiles helps financial and nonfinancial actors remain resilient to changing circumstances.

Fifth, financial markets contribute to price formation and informativeness. Stock prices, interest rates, and other market signals aggregate vast amounts of decentralized information about underlying economic prospects. When these prices reflect fundamental values, capital flows to its most productive uses. However, where informational frictions persist, the market may misprice assets, leading to instability.

Sixth, financial systems provide ways to mitigate incentive alignment problems when there is information asymmetry or agency costs. For example, banks have always had a role to play in managing the imperfect information provided by borrowers, such as the meaningful effort exerted by loan officers to gather soft details. Beyond asymmetric information, principal-agent relationships permeate finance, from shareholders delegating to empire-building managers to retail investors needing advice from honest, unconflicted financial advisors. Through novel contract and security design features, financial service providers help to align incentives.

The financial system provides a foundation for economic activity by fulfilling these six functions. Historically, banks have primarily been responsible for delivering these six functions. Banks were in this privileged position because their business model of taking in deposits and making loans enabled them to provide unique services like payments to the general public that were not as feasible for other business models without the advent of digital tools.

Summarizing these core capabilities enables a broad perspective of FinTech innovation. Namely, any innovation meant to improve or build upon these core financial functions is part of the "FinTech" landscape. From an innovation perspective, Schumpeter (1934) distinguished between five types of innovations, which include (i) new products, (ii) new methods of production, (iii) new sources of supply, (iv) exploitation of new markets, and (v) new business models. What is striking about FinTech startups is that they often combine more than one type of innovation, especially outside of the conventional FinTech realm. For example, blockchain provides a new method of production, which, when combined with smart contracts, enables new business models that arguably have a competitive advantage because they can offer new, customized products or include those traditionally excluded from financial markets.

The transformative potential of FinTech, therefore, should not solely be judged by a single technical merit (e.g., better credit prediction from AI) but rather by its combined capacity to enhance the six core functions of any financial system. It is also true that this powerful interconnectedness among the innovations means that new core capabilities are emerging as part of the system. Given these developments, in the subsequent subsections, I will describe the core technologies underlying FinTech (i.e., AI, blockchain, smart contracts, digital assets, etc.) and their emergent combination (AI × crypto).

This functional perspective also helps explain why a future with potentially novel regulatory solutions may be the appropriate response in the FinTech era. Another unique facet in this era of FinTech innovation is that the innovations have not been limited to new entrants trying to work within the system. Instead, the entrants are trying to build a whole new financial infrastructure, typically on blockchains, rather than improving access to or making the existing traditional system more efficient. By creating a whole new infrastructure, especially one that is open-source and allows anyone to build upon it, the barriers to entry in financial services, such as high fixed costs from compliance, have been dramatically lowered. This, in turn, encourages even more entry and competition, ushering in meaningful change to the financial system. This innovation is typically associated with efficiency gains, yet novel and unpredictable risks, potentially necessitating a new definition of systemic risk (Adrian and Brunnermeier, 2016).

Before I introduce the specific technologies underlying this era of FinTech and data on their prevalence, I want to put their development in historical context, making it easier to see where traditional regulatory solutions for innovation are likely to face challenges.

2.2 Financial Innovation in Historical Context

It is well established that young, high-growth entrepreneurial firms are essential for innovation and economic growth. Indeed, innovation often serves as a competitive advantage for new entrants to gain market share and generate profits in established industries. In addition, regulatory barriers are known to prevent entry or distort prices in such a way as to inhibit entrepreneurship. Historically, the banking industry and the financial system generally have not had as many entrepreneurial entrants as other industrial sectors. Thus, it's essential to understand how financial innovations come about and how much this current wave of innovations differs from prior ones.

Focusing on parallels and divergences in the pattern of financial innovation reveals that in past eras, a single type of innovation in the Schumpeter sense often emerged from incumbents to achieve efficiency gains in core financial capabilities, which contrasts starkly with this era of FinTech innovation. Yet both this era and previous eras of financial innovation seem catalyzed by either cost reductions associated with technological progress or in response to institutional change. Typically, a given technological advance in business methods reduced costs and drove efficiency gains in financial services, and these more efficient practices spread throughout the industry, influencing the overall efficiency. Shifts in the regulatory landscapes only occurred after increased adoption (Tufano, 2003; Lerner and Tufano, 2012). In these cases, financial innovation emerged as a solution to frictions common in financial services, such as high levels of asymmetric information, transaction costs, or tax constraints.

As an example, consider how early financial innovation enabled faster transactions. There is no new product, but rather, there is a new method to produce it. The automated teller machine (ATM) exemplifies this type of early financial innovation, as it significantly transformed retail banking by automating transaction processing and providing convenience to customers. While ATMs reduced transaction costs and improved service accessibility, they reinforced banks' roles rather than displacing them. Next, consider new products, such as a unique way to structure a security (e.g., tax-advantaged municipal bonds) or introducing credit cards. Again, like with ATMs, these products improved service accessibility. In these instances, no new core financial service was offered, and the underlying infrastructure (e.g., banks and intermediaries) remained the same.

Also, typically, these innovations were not the type of invention for which banks would seek IP protection. Thus, while credit cards transformed payment methods, they did not significantly alter the financial infrastructure. Notably, Bank of America issued the first credit card, but there was a belief that early credit cards may not have been considered novel enough for patent protection. Moreover, given the high cost of entry in the financial services industry, most financial institutions relied on other competitive advantages like their existing customer relationships, brand recognition, and distribution networks to fend off competitors. In fact, it was only after the 1998 State Street Bank decision that the financial services industry started to pursue IP protection regularly (Hall, 2009).

From a historical perspective, the current wave of innovation is different for several reasons, but only a few reasons lead to regulatory differences. First, the locus of innovation has moved from banks being the innovators to technology-focused entities and FinTech startups being the innovators (Lerner et al., 2024). This transformation marks a change whereby traditional banks have ceded innovative capabilities to tech-driven newcomers. Part of this may be that this cycle of financial innovation has focused less on business-centric applications and the business method improvements incumbents typically pursued and more on consumer-centric ones, where the user design experience is paramount.

To understand why this distinction alone does not necessitate regulatory differences, consider neobanks. These digital-only startups embody a single type of innovation, that of business model innovation. Neobanks essentially provide a more user-friendly interface to traditional banking services while still operating within the established financial system. Neobanks often use a bank-partnership model. The partner bank holds the deposits and issues the debit cards, while the neobank provides the customer-facing app, technology infrastructure, and customer service. Unlike traditional banks that rely on interest income, neobanks generate revenue through subscription fees for premium services, referral fees for third-party financial products, and fee income from specific services like expedited transfers. In this sense, it is clear that the regulatory scrutiny should focus on where bad actors are likely to engage, such as deceptive marketing practices and the exploitation of behavioral biases. These are all areas where regulators have experience, and the approach parallels easily. Yet most FinTech innovations now encompass multiple innovations in the Schumpeter sense.

Another reason this wave of innovation is different is that information itself has become the central commodity being transacted, not merely a facilitator of a financial exchange. The tension between more efficient information-gathering capabilities and strategic selection of information sets represents an economic trade-off that prior regulatory frameworks have not adequately addressed. When firms can selectively harvest consumer data at near-zero marginal cost, the resulting information asymmetry creates not merely a private advantage but a potential market failure. Similarly, when blockchain-based smart contracts need information external to the smart contract to execute the agreement (e.g., current exchange prices, which oracles can provide), understanding new risks associated with accessing that information (i.e., biased or manipulated representation) is critical. As is explored in Section 3.8, this information issue is central to the emerging FinTech technologies, including AI and blockchain.

Yet another feature that makes this wave of innovation so different is that the innovators are trying to create an entirely new financial infrastructure rather than simply improving access to or reducing friction in the existing system. In this sense, the current wave of financial innovation, which, at times, is trying to replace traditional intermediaries with automated protocols or smart contracts does not have natural regulatory parallels as the markets may provide similar core capabilities, but the infrastructure used to generate the capability doesn't necessarily have the same centralized bottlenecks like a small number of brokers that current regulatory can focus on.

Perhaps, more importantly, and uniquely, this achievement of creating a new infrastructure has been done in a much more open-source way than any past innovation. This is making it a lot easier for anyone to build something new. This also enables customization and composability of financial primitives at an unprecedented scale. When such primitives interconnect in a Lego-like fashion, it allows for new core capabilities to be offered by the financial system (e.g., see my discussion of DAEs and entrepreneurship as a novel service in Section 3.7). By lowering the barriers to entry and innovation, the new financial system will likely be more efficient along some dimensions (e.g., less concentrated, so less rent extraction), yet, at the same time, the ease of entry will attract bad actors and speculators.

Along with technological innovation, institutional forces serve as powerful catalysts for financial innovation by establishing frameworks that shape market behavior and economic activity. An example of institution-driven financial innovation is the development of index funds in the 1970s. They emerged as a direct response to institutional constraints in the investment management industry. Before their creation, the prevailing institutional structure favored active management despite mounting evidence that most active managers failed to outperform market indices after fees. Thus, there was pent-up demand for a cost-effective investment vehicle. Recognizing this inefficiency, Vanguard's founder created the first publicly traded index fund.

This example, however, reinforces the ideas we saw when technological progress rather than institutional changes catalyzed innovation. Early periods of FinTech innovation were characterized by a single type of innovation (typically product or process innovation). They occurred in response to persistent inefficiencies or failure to serve market participants optimally.

However, they never created a new financial system, nor did they combine multiple types of innovation in Schumpeter's sense.

In contrast, recent FinTech innovations introduce novel institutional arrangements and reshape how trust, governance, and control are managed in financial transactions. Unlike previous institutional structures, blockchain technology can reduce reliance on traditional intermediaries. Yet, these decentralized structures pose new regulatory challenges, from definitional questions such as what defines custody to deeper concerns related to accountability, risk management, and financial stability.

Combining AI with blockchain further compounds these complexities by increasing the potential for economic distortions. AI-driven predictive technologies can amplify systemic risks, create market manipulation vulnerabilities, and exacerbate informational asymmetries in these new financial markets. These distortions present challenges distinct from historical precedents, necessitating entirely new regulatory approaches.

Thus, while previous literature has acknowledged the complexity introduced by financial innovation, including its potential for substantial externalities, it does not speak to the specific distortions introduced when integrating multiple types of innovation in the Schumpeterian sense and which AI × crypto applications exemplify. As I argue in this Element, AI and blockchain are integrating, and therefore, it is helpful to view the regulation from an integrated approach. When combined, the economic distortions these technologies create can differ from individual ones, although we can learn from the individual ones. In this sense, the sum of the parts equals more than the parts individually because of these synergies, and new solutions are required to address the unique risks associated with this powerful combination.

2.3 Domains of FinTech Innovation

Below is a high-level overview of the major areas of FinTech that will form the backdrop for this Element and the dataset described below. The classification reflects common market segments and the interplay of emerging technologies with traditional financial services (TradFi).

First, there is conventional FinTech, which focuses on enhancing existing services rather than reinventing them from scratch. For example, peer-to-peer (P2P) lending platforms connect individual borrowers and lenders directly, reducing overhead costs and streamlining loan approvals. Similarly, Buy Now, Pay Later (BNPL) solutions aim to disrupt traditional consumer credit markets by offering short-term installment financing, often at the point of sale. Each of these developments addresses long-standing friction in cost and speed within mainstream finance and is the most similar to the ATM or credit card examples from history. Conventional FinTech shares the most parallels with earlier financial innovations (e.g., ATMs, credit cards) in that they tend to be process or product-oriented and are not recreating new infrastructure outside the traditional financial system, nor are they creating a new financial function.

A second category focuses on applying AI to core financial functions through automation, personalization, and predictive capabilities. AI-powered robo-advisors now provide personalized investment recommendations at a fraction of traditional management fees, democratizing wealth management services. In lending, AI can analyze real-time, big data beyond traditional credit scores to assess risk more accurately, expanding access to credit for underserved populations. Fraud detection systems leverage AI to identify suspicious patterns in real-time, dramatically reducing financial crimes while minimizing false positives that previously created friction for legitimate customers. Meanwhile, LLMs have transformed customer service through intelligent chatbots that handle routine inquiries instantly, allowing human agents to focus on more complex tasks. While AI promises efficiency gains and improved accuracy, it also raises concerns about transparency, data privacy, and potential biases embedded in its models.

A third category focuses on the blockchain and Web3 technologies that underpin cryptocurrencies like Bitcoin and Ethereum, but their use cases extend beyond digital currency. By providing a decentralized, tamper-resistant ledger, blockchain can expedite settlement times, reduce transaction fees, and enable automated smart contracts, which are self-executing code that enforces contract terms without central intermediaries. Digital assets have blossomed beyond simple payment tokens to encompass stablecoins and many other types, each with potentially distinct regulatory considerations (Cong and Xiao, 2021).

DeFi furthers blockchain's potential, constructing financial products like lending, trading, and insurance on open protocols without traditional intermediaries. In DeFi, governance may lie with DAOs, whose rules and operations are encoded in software and collectively decided upon by token holders (Appel and Grennan, 2023). Finally, Web3 components like NFTs introduce digital scarcity into art, collectibles, and real estate. Their unique identifiers mean each token can represent a distinct piece of digital (or physical) property. Soul-bound tokens (SBTs) build on the scarcity introduced with NFTs by serving as identity-bound, nontransferable assets, which are valuable for credentialing or reputation systems.

Finally, an emerging frontier is the fusion of AI with blockchain technologies, which has colloquially been called "AI × Crypto." Early ventures in this domain apply cryptoeconomic frameworks to accelerate AI development. Although major centralized AI providers have dominated the field through economies of scale, new projects are developing decentralized alternatives by experimenting with novel model architectures and incentive platforms. Broadly, four areas define this space: (1) decentralized compute networks offering pooled GPU resources for training and inference as highlighted by Cong et al. (2023g); (2) coordination platforms incentivizing AI model development or enabling specialized inference approaches; (3) DAEs, which are AI agents and related tools and applications that can closely replicate traditional workflows and engage in entrepreneurial endeavors; and (4) decentralized general intelligence (DGI) which aims to produce an application layer similar to what has been put forth by OpenAI and Anthropic, namely, a productized AI solution for consumer or enterprise use.

2.4 Data on FinTech Innovation

To evaluate trends in FinTech innovation, I assembled data on FinTech startup entry from four major providers: Messari, Dove Metrics, Crunchbase, and Preqin – each of which has some advantages and caveats in terms of comprehensive FinTech data on funding, founding dates, and company-level details. For instance, Messari, which later acquired Dove Metrics, has the most comprehensive data on crypto startups, including unofficial announcements of funding via Twitter. Crunchbase and Preqin are more traditional sources of data for startups. Preqin has some of the most comprehensive fundraising data, but this gives it a bias toward firms that receive at least some VC funding, whereas Crunchbase typically has details even on young startups that may not have raised meaningful capital yet. By harmonizing across these sources, I aim to provide a more complete view of both traditional venture-funded startups (the standard route for conventional FinTechs), and those financed through more novel mechanisms, such as token-based financing. Online Appendix A details the initial aggregation.

To classify the startup's business description into one of the FinTech domains, I employ a multistep classification procedure. The four categories or domains include traditional FinTechs, AI, Blockchain, and AI × Crypto. This process began with targeted keyword searches (e.g., blockchain, artificial intelligence, stablecoin, etc.) and was subsequently refined using large-language-model (LLM) filters tailored to identify nuanced business model references. Finally, I conduct manual checks for borderline or ambiguous cases, resulting in the final dataset. This multi-step approach balances scalability and rigor, enabling a detailed analysis of domain-level patterns while maintaining a high degree of classification accuracy. For the exact keywords and prompts used to classify, please see Online Appendix A.

2.5 Summary Statistics

Figure 1 provides a high-level view of how total disclosed FinTech fundraising has evolved worldwide and in the U.S. from 2012 through 2024. Globally, the total amount of capital raised that has been publicly disclosed has grown markedly over this period across all four subcategories of FinTech innovation:

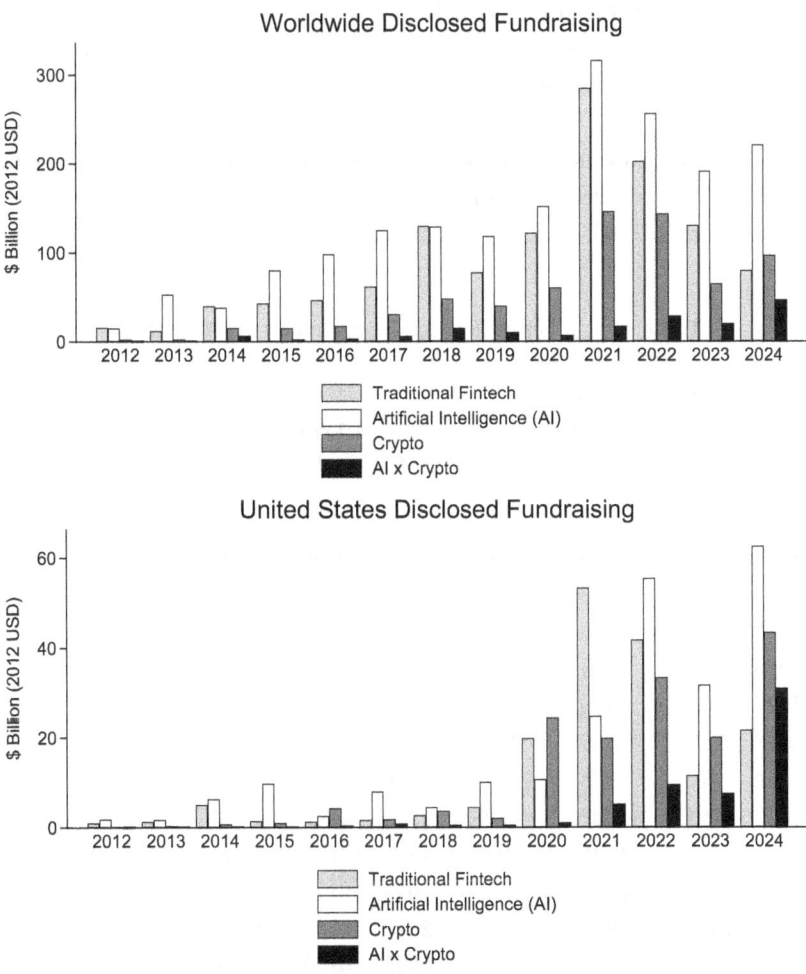

Figure 1 Total disclosed FinTech fundraising (2012–2024). The figures depict the total disclosed FinTech fundraising globally and in the United States from 2012 through 2024. The business models of the funded startups are categorized into Traditional FinTech, AI, Crypto, and AI × Crypto.

traditional FinTech, AI, crypto, and combined AI × crypto. Yet the relative contribution of each category diverges over time. In the early 2010s, funding was dominated by more conventional FinTech business models focused on payments, peer-to-peer lending, and robo-advising, while AI- and crypto-focused ventures initially raised only modest amounts. By the late 2010s and into the early 2020s, however, AI and crypto reached parity or surpassed traditional FinTech startups in terms of total funding, signaling an inflection point in investor preferences. Although starting from a small base, the AI × crypto segment displays especially rapid growth, reflecting demand for solutions that integrate these technologies. Notably, although U.S. fundraising volume is proportionally smaller than global totals, it echoes the same upward trajectory and category shifts, highlighting the prominent role of U.S.-based startups in shaping FinTech innovation despite meaningful regulatory uncertainty and related challenges.

Turning from the aggregate funding trends documented in Figures 2 to the specific startup counts, Table 1 provides a breakdown of the number of unique startups funded each year in the U.S. and globally between 2012 and 2024.

Table 1 Number of FinTech startups funded (2012–2024)

Year	Trad. FinTech Global	Trad. FinTech U.S.	AI Global	AI U.S.	Crypto Global	Crypto U.S.	AI × Crypto Global	AI × Crypto U.S.
2012	760	189	1069	189	1586	800	75	32
2013	980	243	1468	261	2393	1108	126	50
2014	1553	382	2158	367	3364	1509	227	88
2015	2274	395	3358	443	4622	1803	382	138
2016	2585	404	4144	549	5147	1637	564	181
2017	3116	466	5388	736	5964	1823	837	264
2018	3769	659	6513	879	7172	2231	1075	327
2019	3976	676	7328	989	7690	2305	1332	391
2020	4453	802	7983	1215	8206	2714	1452	456
2021	7317	1635	10401	1838	14133	5018	2252	785
2022	6322	1337	9420	1694	10175	3138	2040	666
2023	4421	915	9708	2247	8217	2588	2320	859
2024	3515	656	8398	1843	6143	1739	1819	665

Note: This table shows the number of unique startups funded each year across four FinTech subfields: traditional FinTech, AI, Crypto, and AI × Crypto. Both global and U.S.-specific counts are provided.

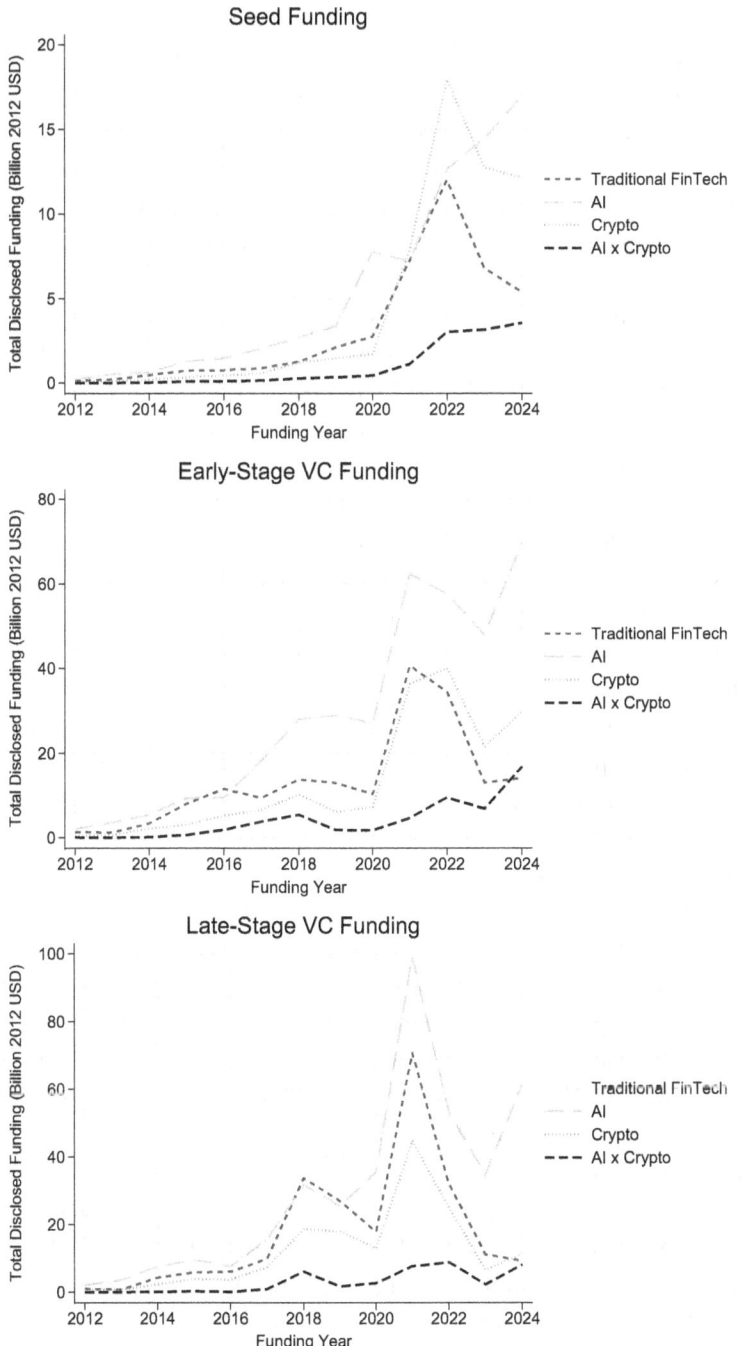

Figure 2 Total disclosed FinTech fundraising by stage (2012–2024). The figures depict the total disclosed FinTech fundraising by stage of startup (seed funding, early-stage, or late-stage funding) for the global sample from 2012 through 2024. The business models of the funded startups are categorized into Traditional FinTech, AI, Crypto, and AI × Crypto.

Again, the counts are disaggregated by the four subcategories of FinTech innovation. In addition, the columns are further broken out by global versus U.S. totals. The data reveals several trends. First, traditional FinTech and AI startups show the largest absolute increases over time, reflecting the continued maturation of these technologies worldwide. Second, crypto-focused ventures exhibit a marked rise from modest beginnings in the early 2010s to increasingly substantial numbers by the mid-2020s, coinciding with the broadening of crypto into DeFi and other applications. Importantly, from a regulatory perspective, the AI × crypto category, although starting from a relatively low base, displays a steep upward trajectory both within the U.S. and globally. This latter observation highlights the growing convergence of AI-driven and blockchain-based innovations in the FinTech sector. This trend, along with other parallels between the branches of FinTech, requires a more integrated regulatory framework rather than separate oversight. Finally, the U.S. numbers, in particular, indicate that policymakers must be prepared to handle the compound challenges posed by AI × crypto startups, given the rapidly expanding presence of these startups and their revealed preference for U.S. locations.

Next, I explore a more granular view of how funding flows vary by startup maturity. Figures 2 and 3 break down publicly disclosed FinTech fundraising into seed, early-stage VC, and late-stage VC categories. These figures build upon the startup counts provided in Table 1 by clarifying not only how many ventures are funded in each subsector but also how heavily they are financed at different points in their life cycles, which helps assess the sector's trajectory and the potential regulatory touchpoints.

Figure 2 focuses on global trends and reveals that, although seed-stage funding for traditional FinTech dominated early in the sample, AI startups commanded an increasing share of early-stage and late-stage funding by the late 2010s. Crypto investments, while initially small, gained momentum in the early 2020s, with AI × Crypto showing growth during the seed and early-stage rounds after 2020. For example, in 2023–2024, AI × Crypto exhibits near-parity with traditional AI in certain stages, suggesting enthusiasm for combined AI × Crypto solutions.

Figure 3 shows an analogous breakdown for U.S. startups, tracing similar patterns but with some notable differences in the relative magnitudes across subsectors. Seed funding for U.S. AI ventures, for instance, accelerated significantly around 2021 and overtook Traditional FinTech by 2022. Crypto and AI × Crypto remains smaller in the seed stage than globally, but has surged more prominently in early- and late-stage rounds, indicating that U.S.

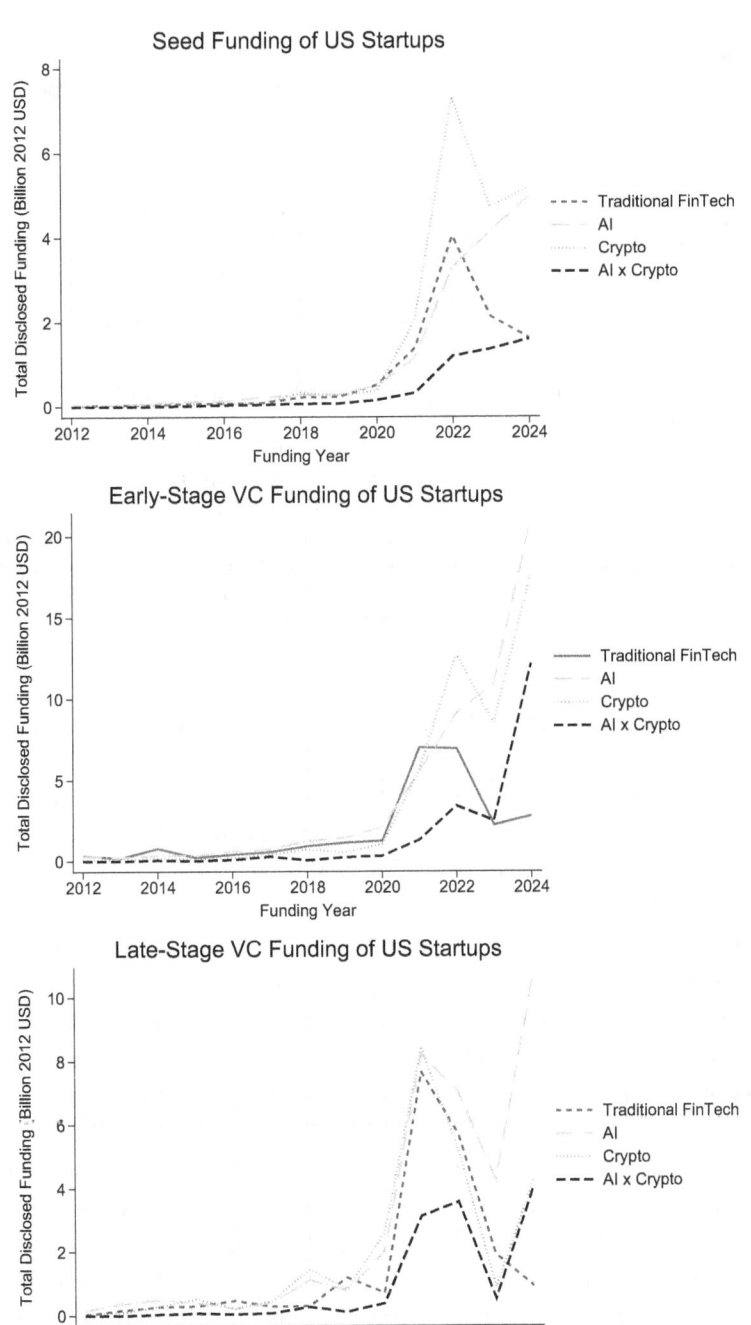

Figure 3 U.S. FinTech funding by stage of startup (2012–2024). The figures depict the total disclosed FinTech fundraising by stage of startup (seed funding, early-stage, or late-stage funding) for the U.S. sample from 2012 through 2024. The business models of the funded startups are categorized into Traditional FinTech, AI, Crypto, and AI × Crypto.

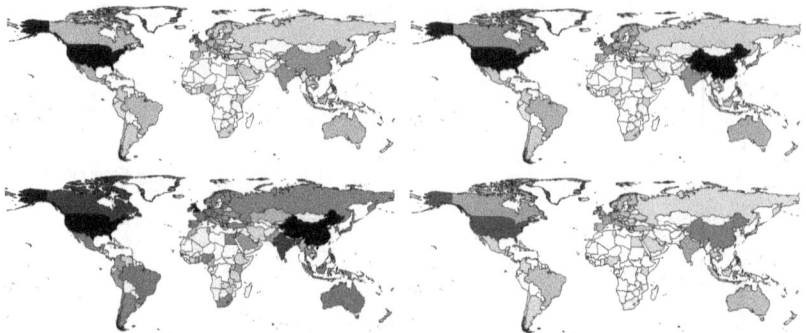

Figure 4 Heatmap of FinTech firms globally by subcategory. The figures depict the total unique FinTech firms by country. The firm's business model has been categorized into traditional FinTech, artificial intelligence (AI), crypto, and AI × crypto. The green figure represents traditional FinTech (upper left). The red figure AI (lower left). The blue figure crypto (upper right), and the purple figure AI × crypto (lower right). The darker the color, the greater the concentration of startups. The color gradient moves from lightest to darkest with breaks at 1, 10, 20, 50, 200, 1000, 2000, 5000, and 30000 firms.

investors place a heightened emphasis on scaling ventures in these emerging technologies.

When comparing global versus U.S. trends, the principal divergence lies in the timing and intensity of early-stage investments in AI × Crypto, with dramatic spikes in recent years in the U.S. compared to more moderate increases globally. This suggests that the U.S. continues to play a dominant role in nurturing advanced FinTech innovation and startups, despite regulatory uncertainty. A second trend in the figures is that investor attention is shifting from smaller seed bets in toward more substantial later-stage commitments for narrowly focused innovations (e.g., either AI or crypto in isolation), reinforcing the need to develop cohesive regulatory structures that can adapt to the scaling FinTech ecosystem.

Building on the stage-specific insights provided by Figures 3 and 4, Table 2 provides a complementary perspective by detailing average funding round sizes (in millions of 2012 U.S. dollars) for each FinTech subcategory across seed, early-stage VC, late-stage VC, and token sale rounds. While overall funding amounts in seed rounds have grown notably over time (particularly for AI-focused ventures), early-stage and late-stage VC categories account for the largest share of capital, which makes sense since much of the ecosystem hinges on scaling established startups rather than seeding new entrants.

Table 2 Average funding round sixe for FinTech startups

Year	Trad. FinTech Seed	Trad. FinTech Early-Stage	Trad. FinTech Late-Stage	AI Seed	AI Early-Stage	AI Late-Stage	Crypto Seed	Crypto Early-Stage	Crypto Late-Stage	Crypto Token Sale	AI × Crypto Seed	AI × Crypto Early-Stage	AI × Crypto Late-Stage	AI × Crypto Token Sale
2012	1	10	23	1	8	20	1	8	37	–	1	9	7	–
2013	1	7	18	1	11	26	1	10	30	2	1	5	13	–
2014	2	12	63	1	11	41	1	21	66	0	1	10	23	–
2015	2	21	61	2	14	46	1	18	70	0	1	14	28	0
2016	2	31	53	2	13	40	1	24	80	9	1	31	16	9
2017	2	20	74	2	18	58	2	22	121	35	1	44	70	35
2018	2	24	213	2	24	101	2	32	204	140	2	64	243	15
2019	3	20	129	2	22	67	3	16	170	47	2	16	60	6
2020	3	16	84	5	18	80	2	17	110	6	2	15	81	6
2021	4	35	181	3	29	134	3	38	183	6	2	20	111	6
2022	5	32	114	4	27	106	4	34	135	5	3	29	117	15
2023	4	23	86	4	29	102	3	25	74	4	3	21	80	1
2024	4	25	93	6	48	197	4	42	140	3	4	67	225	2

Note: This table shows the average funding round size in $ millions of 2012 USD across four FinTech subfields: traditional FinTech, AI, Crypto, and AI × Crypto. These are global numbers.

Late-stage AI deals, in particular, stand out from 2018 onward, indicative of investor confidence in the potential for AI solutions to mature and expand. By contrast, Crypto and AI × crypto rounds, while experiencing phases of dramatic growth, display a more volatile pattern, potentially reflecting the still-evolving regulatory uncertainties they face.

The inclusion of token sale funding highlights another important way FinTech startups can raise funds for their business. Although ICOs achieved notoriety between 2017 and 2018 due to a slew of fraudulent offerings before falling out of favor, particularly in U.S. markets, due to intensifying regulatory scrutiny (Lyandres and Rabetti, 2023). Nevertheless, the data indicate that private and public token sales continue to provide capital for crypto startups worldwide. This underscores the continued importance of token-based fundraising for specific segments of the FinTech community, and it aligns with a need to rethink optimal approaches to regulating token sales.

Finally, building upon the preceding analyses of funding dynamics, Figure 4 offers a geographic perspective on FinTech startups by illustrating the global distribution of unique FinTech startups in each subcategory with traditional FinTech in green, AI in blue, crypto in red, and AI × crypto in purple. Each panel employs a color gradient, where darker shades indicate a higher concentration of startups, with thresholds ranging from 1 to 30,000 ventures. This visual representation accentuates the extent to which certain countries have become FinTech hubs, revealing both macro-level dominance and subcategory-specific strengths.

Two countries, the U.S. and China, display dense footprints across nearly all FinTech subfields. India, the United Kingdom, and Canada emerge as significant second-tier centers, outpacing most other regions in terms of FinTech startups. Russia, Singapore, and Brazil are also highlighted by darker gradients in specific subcategories, indicating entrepreneurial strength, albeit focused a somewhat narrower set of specific FinTech applications like crypto. Interestingly, the transition from conventional FinTech to the most recent AI × Crypto wave reveals subtle yet important shifts in geographic clustering. While numerous European countries exhibit some depth in AI or Crypto individually, the U.S. stands out for its incredibly high concentration of AI × Crypto startups, surpassing China and all other countries in this combined category while being on par in individual categories like AI. This suggests that the U.S. may occupy a relatively advanced position in integrating AI and blockchain innovations, reflective of a confluence of capital availability, technological expertise, and entrepreneurial dynamics that collectively shape its FinTech landscape.

3 The Economics of FinTech Growth (Present)

The empirical evidence demonstrates substantial capital allocation and entrepreneurial activity across various FinTech domains. This pattern of investment and innovation raises a fundamental question: What economic forces are driving the development and adoption of these technologies? Building on the historical examples illustrating that financial innovation typically occurs in response to cost reductions brought about by technological progress or in response to institutional change, this section overviews the economic factors propelling innovation, adoption, and entry in various FinTech domains.

First, I provide a brief background on the institutional factors contributing to the supply and demand dynamics that has led to this era of FinTech innovations before subsequently diving into the details of specific cost-reducing technologies, including conventional FinTech applications (3.2), AI (3.3), blockchain, digital assets, and smart contracts (3.4), DeFi and DAOs (3.5), NFTs and SBTs (3.6), and finally, AI × crypto (3.7). The section concludes by reviewing the common economic themes that emerged regardless of the specific technology. Examining these forces helps to isolate the common economic distortions for which standard regulatory solutions exist, like price regulation or a firm's entry and exit decisions. The review also helps clarify the extent to which unusual or novel distortions are arising that may necessitate new regulatory solutions.

3.1 The Supply and Demand Dynamics Driving FinTech Growth

The 2008 financial crisis is the primary institutional catalyst for the current era of FinTech innovation. The crisis revealed substantial shortcomings in regulation, highlighting how financial oversight struggled to keep pace with financial innovation, which was mostly centered around new products (e.g., new forms of securitization). This gap incentivized change through both necessity and opportunity. It prompted the development of new regulatory frameworks, entrepreneurial entry by FinTech startups, and questioning the financial system's core risk management capability.

Specifically, in the 2008 financial crisis aftermath, a paradigm shift occurred in financial innovation, marking what, in retrospect, is the genesis of the modern FinTech era. The financial crisis shifted supply and demand. Namely, it increased the supply of talent working on financial inefficiencies and fundamentally changed the features consumers and investors demanded from their financial services providers. By exposing structural vulnerabilities within the traditional financial system, the crisis catalyzed both sides to realize that fundamental reforms were needed. Notably, given that certain financial innovations had contributed to systemic instability, there was a recognition that subsequent technological advancements would require a different approach.

On the supply side, this post-crisis environment reawakened those associated with the cyberpunk movement to work on solving the peer-to-peer money challenge. While many of the original pieces were there, it was the seminal whitepaper by Nakamoto (2008), which introduced Bitcoin as a decentralized alternative to conventional financial infrastructure, and drew technical and engineering talent to financial system inefficiencies. The entrepreneurial talent in the high-tech sector started to reorient its expertise from cryptography and electrical engineering toward financial frictions and shortcomings of the system, therefore, it represents a defining characteristic of modern FinTech.

The financial crisis, however, did more than just shift talent. The 2008–2009 financial crisis, triggered by innovations in mortgage securitization, provides a stark illustration of how complexity and opacity can enable systemic risks to accumulate undetected. Securitization, which bundled residential mortgages into tradable securities, was initially designed to spread risk and lower borrowing costs. However, as Griffin (2021) documents, this innovation became a vehicle for systemic risk due to pervasive misreporting, fraud, and conflicts of interest among key players. The complexity of these instruments obscured underlying risks while creating incentives for originators to extend credit to borrowers unable to sustain their loans.

This crisis experience shaped the subsequent FinTech revolution through a demand channel. First, the erosion of trust in traditional financial institutions created the demand for more trustworthy institutions. As such, business models emphasizing transparency and decentralization of power became more popular. Bitcoin's introduction in 2008 explicitly positioned itself as a response to the crisis, offering a trustless, peer-to-peer financial system that would eliminate the need for potentially unreliable intermediaries. Second, increased regulatory oversight forced some banks to reduce traditional lending post-crisis. This created market opportunities for financial innovations that could improve access to financial services for these marginalized groups in a manner akin to the ATMs and credit cards of early innovation eras. For example, new platforms emerged to fill gaps in credit markets, with crowdfunding and peer-to-peer lending offering alternatives to traditional intermediation. Third, the 2008 financial crisis highlighted the importance of better risk assessment and monitoring tools. This demand for better intelligence, coupled with the massive cost reductions attributable to digitization, made it easy for executives to justify investments in the technologies that incorporate big data and advanced AI.

What are the massive cost reductions brought about by digitization? As Goldfarb and Tucker (2019) delineate, five cost changes came about because of digital technologies' capacity to encode information as bits. Digitization reduces search, replication, transportation, tracking, and verification costs. This, combined with Moore's law and Kryder's law, which respectively posit the exponential growth of processing power and storage capacity, meant that computation and storage costs also declined. In such a state, it is natural to see an increase in the supply of applications using computationally intensive cryptographic proofs or big-data-driven AI algorithms.

3.2 Conventional FinTech Applications

Conventional FinTech applications, including digital payments, credit expansion via BNPL, peer-to-peer lending, and crowdfunding, are part of the first wave of FinTech innovations. Typically, traditional FinTech founders and innovators create a competitive advantage by introducing economic benefits such as reduced transaction costs and increased accessibility. However, these features that attract customers often pose novel regulatory challenges. For example, regulators face new concerns about consumer privacy and exploiting vulnerable populations. Despite conventional FinTech applications being incremental iterations of financial products and services that regulators are familiar with, the dilemmas they pose to regulators are similar to those brought about by more radical innovations like AI and DeFi. Therefore, a higher-level view of the economics of these conventional FinTech applications helps provide a valuable analogue to the economic issues that regulators face with the more radical innovations.

First, consider digital payments, which enable instant, remote transactions between two parties. These digital payments raise new privacy risks that do not exist with cash or traditional credit cards. Payment system operators can now collect detailed data on individual consumer purchases, including item-level data on what was bought, where, and when. This data can be combined with personal information like phone numbers, email addresses, and home addresses to build detailed profiles of consumers' lives. Consumers are concerned about these infringements on their privacy, and over time, they have come to oppose their data being collected and shared (Goldfarb and Tucker, 2012). Thus, a rationale for regulatory intervention in this setting is typically not about alleviating a specific constraint or distortion but about following the broad guiding principle of ensuring privacy. Thus, from a high-level perspective, it is worth evaluating how different ensuring privacy in payments is from settings like Meta's more revolutionary attempt at a stablecoin or AI innovators' decisions to include private data for training their models. Perhaps, surprisingly, the underlying economics are not that different.

At a high level, many U.S. laws and regulations encourage intervention if deception occurs. Now, consider this analogy. Just like large retail corporations cannot advertise a sale on TVs for $100 but only have one in stock, then lead the consumer who tried to buy the $100 TV to buy another similar yet much more expensive TV, in the FinTech context, startups should not be allowed to advertise convenience only to lead users to products that feature convenience bundled with data extraction, which is much more expensive to consumers. It is a classic bait-and-switch that exploits the underlying psychology of consumers. The lower advertised price "baits" the consumers, then the salesperson or AI-recommendation app "switches" the consumer to a higher-priced item. Therefore, users need to realize that whether it is a conventional FinTech application or a new Web3 application, some developers are attempting to deceive them, so they should exercise caution.

Insights from behavioral economics help to explain why consumers are vulnerable (Kahneman, 2013). Consumers are more likely to trust new products and services when they are easier to understand. New technology often provides intuitive, user-friendly interfaces that make it easy for consumers to adopt without deep thinking. Yet thinking through the risks of using such technology requires one to allocate attention to effortful mental activities and make complex calculations (e.g., my probability of being a victim of a cybercrime from sharing my data). However, the Federal Trade Commission (FTC) has long classified certain deceptive or unfair advertising practices and prohibits violating those advertising rules. Since 1968, the FTC has not permitted bait-and-switch advertising. Typically, if the FTC takes action against a company for false advertising, they are likely to issue a cease-and-desist order, and in some cases, to go a step further and require that the company engage in corrective advertising, in which the company explicitly states that the former advertising claims were untrue. Thus, one potential regulatory solution could be to go through the FTC and encourage FinTech startups to stop doing this and engage in corrective advertising that would serve a FinTech literacy role. FinTech literacy as a regulatory solution is discussed in greater detail in Section 5.

Next, consider a similar scenario with a mobile payment app that enables purchases with a single tap, and a proposed regulatory solution in California. The payments app collects data on every transaction, including what was purchased, where, and when. The app uses this data to provide personalized recommendations and offers, enhancing the user's shopping experience. From an economic perspective, the convenience provided by the app is valuable. It saves time, simplifies budgeting, and offers tailored discounts, making the shopping process more efficient and providing users with higher utility. Psychologically, the user is driven by the ease of use and immediate benefits. The app's interface is designed to be intuitive, requiring minimal effort to operate. The instant gratification of quick payments and personalized deals appeals to the user's present bias. The user might also trust the app due to its association with a reputable brand, reinforcing their willingness to share personal data.

What did California regulators do when faced with a trade-off between enabling the growth of efficient digital payment systems and protecting consumer privacy? California implemented an outright ban, as outlined in the Song-Beverly Credit Card Act. The parallel from that Act would be to prohibit payment systems and merchants from requiring or requesting personal information as part of payment transactions, unless the consumer affirmatively opts in. This would preserve the privacy status quo from the cash/credit card era and maintain a level playing field across payment types. However, it could slow the adoption of digital payments because specific business models would not be viable without the ability to monetize consumer data. In this sense, startup entry would be lower with such bans, which could reduce overall consumer welfare. Thus, if one wants to preserve entrepreneurial entry, a solution based on FinTech literacy may be more appealing.

Another area of innovation in payments brought about by FinTech companies is BNPL, which is a form of short-term consumer credit that allows users to split purchases into installment payments, often with minimal or no fees if paid on time. BNPL has seen explosive growth in recent years, with transaction volumes rising from $33 billion in 2019 to an estimated $120 billion in 2021. This growth has been driven by increasing adoption by both consumers and merchants. From a consumer perspective, BNPL can help alleviate liquidity constraints and smooth consumption. By allowing consumers to break up payments over time with limited upfront commitment, BNPL can make purchases more affordable, especially for those with limited savings or credit access. Consistent with this, Balyuk and Williams (2023) find that liquidity-constrained consumers are more likely to use BNPL and that BNPL access facilitates expenditure smoothing around income shocks.

However, BNPL also carries risks of encouraging overspending and leading to debt accumulation, especially among younger and lower-income users. Maggio et al. (2023) show that BNPL access increases spending levels for all consumers, even those not liquidity-constrained. They argue this is hard to explain with standard intertemporal substitution motives. It is more consistent with the "liquidity flypaper effect" where the additional retail liquidity from BNPL sticks where it hits, fueling short-term spending.

From the merchant's perspective, offering BNPL as a payment option can significantly boost sales. Berg et al. (2023) conduct a randomized experiment with a large e-commerce retailer and find that the mere availability of a BNPL option at checkout increases sales by approximately 20 percent. The spending response to BNPL availability is much larger than to the availability of other payment methods like PayPal. Interestingly, Berg et al. (2023) find that the merchant's profits from increased sales facilitated by BNPL outweigh initial costs in terms of consumer defaults, helping to rationalize the rapid merchant adoption of BNPL. However, to the extent that the market becomes saturated and BNPL becomes so ubiquitous that it leads to defaults, the long-run gains may not be so advantageous.

Thus, like we saw with payments and regulators' difficulty in achieving a broad mission of ensuring privacy when behavioral economics is considered, behavioral responses to BNPL suggest regulatory challenges. In the long run, evidence indicates the potential for welfare-reducing overconsumption, increased defaults, and worse credit in equilibrium. For consumers facing liquidity constraints, the additional purchasing power and flexibility of BNPL can smooth consumption and improve welfare. However, the same features may induce some consumers to overspend in ways that ultimately reduce welfare. For merchants, the sales boost from BNPL can outweigh the costs, unless defaults and other risks are poorly managed. From a regulatory perspective, regulators must grapple with the counterfactual. BNPL is far from first best because of behavioral tendencies, but it may be superior to a counterfactual of payday lending. Moreover, regulatory interventions that may require segmenting populations based on their behavior are complex, often leading to framing solutions like opt-out versus opt-in, rather than one-size-fits-all information disclosures.

Third, consider P2P lending platforms, which offer the potential to expand access to credit by enabling direct matching of borrowers and lenders via online marketplaces. P2P lending can serve borrowers who struggle to get loans from traditional banks. They may also offer better rates to borrowers and higher returns to lenders by reducing overhead costs and enabling more granular risk-based pricing. However, P2P lending raises concerns around credit risk, investor protection, and fair lending compliance. Current P2P platforms make minimal disclosures to lenders about how loans are underwritten. Lenders may not understand the risks they are taking on. There are also concerns P2P lenders could bypass consumer protection laws and enable predatory lending or unfair discrimination using non-traditional data.

Regulators must balance the goal of expanding access to credit against the need to protect potentially vulnerable lenders and borrowers. Overly restrictive regulations could eliminate the cost advantages of P2P lending. However, under-regulation risks enabling excessively risky or abusive lending practices. One approach could be to subject P2P platforms to disclosure and oversight requirements similar to traditional consumer lending, including standardized reporting, usury limits, ability-to-repay rules, and fair lending audits. This would create a more level playing field. However, it may increase the costs of running the platform and reduce the supply of credit that such platforms provide.

Another option would be to limit investment to sophisticated or accredited investors, reducing risks to vulnerable lenders. However, this would cut off P2P lending as an investment option for most households. Therefore, like with BNPL, targeted protection is needed for vulnerable populations, but targeting is often tricky. One potential solution discussed in 5 is RegTech, which would involve incorporating regulatory solutions directly into the product or service so that regulators can provide some form of protection or have knowledge to prevent systemic risk from excessively risky lending. Another might be the adoption of industry codes of conduct, which limit the exploitation of vulnerable populations, or if a startup wants to do business with such populations, requiring registration similar to what payday lenders must do.

Next, consider that some regulatory challenges conventional FinTech poses are nearly identical to well-established regulatory challenges in financial services. Consider crowdfunding, which reduces the cost of entrepreneurs accessing capital. Crowdfunding platforms, like Kickstarter, allow individuals to raise funds from many people via online campaigns. Compared to traditional early-stage financial resources for entrepreneurs, crowdfunding offers some benefits. It lowers search costs by providing a centralized marketplace where creators can pitch directly to a large pool of potential funders. It mitigates geographic constraints, allowing creators to access funding from anywhere globally. Further, receiving crowdfunding provides a new set of signals, like the number of backers, funding raised, and social media engagement, that can help founders, funders, and future investors assess quality.

However, crowdfunding also creates regulatory challenges because it is especially prone to distortions from information asymmetry and, to a lesser extent, behavioral economics (e.g., herding behavior). Investors on the crowdfunding platform often have limited information about creators' true ability or intent to deliver, making it hard to screen for low-quality or even fraudulent campaigns. Agrawal et al. (2014) determine that this can lead to a market for lemons problem (Akerlof, 1970). In particular, adverse selection drives high-quality projects toward traditional financing with stronger signaling mechanisms, while moral hazard incentivizes crowdfunding projects to exaggerate their prospects or misappropriate funds post-financing. Moreover, given that investors usually do not obtain formal control rights, this reduces incentives to monitor creators post-funding, which is one of the major benefits of traditional early-stage financing sources like VC (Hellmann and Puri, 2002; Eldar and Grennan, 2023).

So what can be done? Strausz (2017) demonstrates that properly designed platforms can mitigate these distortions through conditional pledging mechanisms that enable consumers to implement deferred payments, thereby controlling entrepreneurial moral hazard. Other regulatory responses to these market failures have evolved along a common financial regulatory path, with policymakers requiring graduated disclosures and enforcing investment limits. The empirical evidence suggests this regulatory framework creates a complementary role for crowdfunding alongside traditional financing sources rather than a substitute relationship. For example, Chang (2020) shows that a fixed funding mechanism, where money is refunded if funding goals aren't met, makes crowdfunding attractive to resource-constrained startups and established firms. Enabling these solutions affirms what practitioners have witnessed in the decades since crowdfunding was first introduced. Namely, better contracts and proper regulation in crowdfunding markets have enhanced efficiency by reducing demand uncertainty, allowing resources to be allocated to projects that might otherwise remain unfunded due to information frictions in traditional financing services.

To see the analogy between conventional FinTech and more radical innovations like crypto and AI, consider the parallels between crowdfunding and initial coin offerings (ICOs). ICOs allow entrepreneurs to raise funds through token sales, which may grant token holders various rights such as access to a future product, platform, or a share of profits (Lyandres and Rabetti, 2023). Howell et al. (2020) show that ICOs are an effective mechanism for financing growth, with companies that raise more funding in their ICO seeing higher post-ICO employment and valuations. Lyandres et al. (2022) further find that an ICO's success, again measured by the amount raised, positively correlates with survival and future financing. At the same time, ICOs also carry significant risks for investors (Lee et al., 2021). Many ICOs have proven to be scams or failed to deliver their promised products and services. The lack of standardized disclosures and oversight in ICO markets can make it difficult for investors to distinguish high-quality from low-quality projects. As discussed later, regulators have brought significant litigation and enforcement cases over whether tokens are securities that should be subject to the securities law.

In many ways, ICOs can be seen as crowdfunding with added risks. Why? ICOs leverage blockchain technology and tokenization to streamline issuing and trading of a novel type of "hybrid" security with some equity and debt-like features while introducing new and poorly understood risks, such as perverse incentives caused by early liquidity for founders and developer teams. Like other innovations in the conventional FinTech space, there could be benefits from ICOs, but determining how to protect tokenholders is hard. A good first start is to draw upon crowdfunding solutions like graduated regulatory frameworks, contractual solutions, enhanced disclosure requirements, and investment limits, all of which appear to help preserve the benefits of innovation without negative consequences. What will be interesting for regulators and lawyers is to consider the additional implications and risks that emerge from the combination of liquidity, price discovery, and programmable contracts. For example, many token issuers and users are learning that tokens with high fully diluted valuations and low initial circulating supplies can fall into zones that prohibit real progress on the development of the project and ecosystem.

Thus, while these conventional FinTech innovations may, at first glance, appear to operate through different mechanisms than AI or crypto, they are very similar. Conventional FinTech innovations increase access to financial services but also introduce nontrivial risks. Some economic distortions introduced by conventional FinTech are common challenges associated with informational asymmetry, for which well-established solutions exist. Other challenges, like privacy and exploitation of vulnerable populations, will require alternative solutions. However, there are many familiar solutions once the economic changes brought about by the innovation are appropriately framed. For example, regulations can be embedded into the point-of-sale through RegTech or more conventional pathways, such as using the FTC and making counter-advertising or FinTech literacy part of the penalty paid to the FTC. In each case, regulatory solutions are possible and made more evident by understanding the evolution and institutional context that preceded the innovation in the first place.

3.3 AI

Advances in AI are helping to decrease the cost of prediction and exploration (Agrawal et al., 2018). Reinforcement learning (RL), a sub-area of AI, allows agents to learn behaviors in an unknown environment by finding a balance between exploring uncharted territory and exploiting current knowledge. Modern LLMs use RL via RL from Human Feedback (RLHF), which has become a standard technique for aligning LLMs with human preferences and intentions. This approach is valuable for tasks with complex or ill-defined goals, such as determining what makes a response helpful or aligned with ethical values. Agentic AI combines RL with LLMs to create systems that can respond to unforeseen situations while adhering to basic rules and constraints. In this sense, RL teaches optimized writer and critic agents to refine the same output through repeated interaction. This back-and-forth, which can involve two or many agents, enables chain-of-thought reasoning. Thus, AI's capability moves from simply predicting the next word to accurately predicting the type of judgment needed to interpret complex or ill-defined instructions.

Together, this set of cost reductions may encourage incumbents to substitute other inputs, such as labor for AI, as part of the production process. Similarly, reductions in prediction and exploration costs increase the value of complements, such as owning data, and of humans' nonpredictive, nonexploratory skills, such as persuasion and social-emotional skills (Cao et al., 2022; Grennan and Michaely, 2022). This theme of complementary skills implies that AI is a skills-biased tool. While AI can augment productivity, it favors experts with more expansive job skills. For example, a study of managers found that AI benefits the likeable yet incompetent manager, does little to improve the likeable and competent manager's performance, and significantly reduces the perceived performance of the competent jerk (John et al., 2024).

Decreases in the cost of producing predictions or allowing exploration also bring about more subtle yet unintended consequences for labor markets. Consider how much easier it is to improve resumes with AI tools and to send multiple applications. Evidence from the gig labor site, Upwork, shows that post-ChatGPT, there was an increase in applications per job. In the deluge of applicants, the high-quality freelancers who saw themselves getting less recognition adjusted their application strategy by applying to fewer jobs and tailoring themselves to specific skill niches to differentiate themselves relative to their prior behavior (Yiu et al., 2024). In contrast, an expansion in the data provided on tech workers' productivity (i.e., Github's choice to display private domain commits, not just public ones) and thereby, the ability of employers to use AI to screen potential applicants productivity in greater detail, enabled positive assortive matching in the labor market (Gupta et al., 2024).

An economic consideration related to AI is privacy and the many data sources used by AI to train its prediction models, including alternative ones. As researchers search for ways to improve AI's predictive accuracy, they collect data that humans generally would not want to reveal. Moreover, data collection and ensuring data integrity can be costly. For instance, researchers are creating annotated data sets with "visible thoughts" where humans describe what they thought would happen, what they believe is about to happen, what they are paying attention to, where the current sources of tension are in a situation, and so on. The goal of collecting data on annotated thoughts is to add an intermediary chain-of-thought prediction layer that helps to create more accurate AI-generated content. Yet, in making this data, the human advantages brought about by obfuscation are diminished. Suppose data with transparent thoughts were the key to more accurate predictions. In that case, it is possible that many researchers would attempt to collect such data, and inevitably, the data could be used to exploit that person's emotional and psychological vulnerabilities. For example, antitrust scholars are concerned about using such data for price discrimination (Asker et al., 2022). Treating these models as if they understand meaning is challenging from a regulatory perspective because they are only sophisticated pattern-matching systems. At the same time, assigning liability to developers is equally fraught with challenges, suggesting that potentially new models of regulation, perhaps akin to those applied to animals, make more sense (for a detailed discussion, see Section 4.3).

Finally, it's worth recognizing that the consequences of lower prediction costs can appear subtle but amplified through repetition. For example, AI is weak at predicting rare probability events such as tail events. In addition, AI is much more accurate at predicting events in the near future than in the distant future (Dessaint et al., 2024). This tension across horizons may have unexpected consequences for innovation and capital allocation, key drivers of economic growth and consumer welfare. Consider consumer-facing industries, which may fall into the trap of using predictive AI to suggest iterative product improvements rather than exploratory AI to find new products. As Henry Ford famously said before the introduction of the first car, if you were to ask consumers what they want, they would tell you a faster horse. Predictive AI models are much more likely to offer incremental near-term solutions, although AI agents could encourage more creative solutions through the reduced cost of exploration.

3.4 Blockchain, Digital Assets, and Smart Contracts

Advances in blockchain are helping to decrease the cost of state verification (Yermack, 2017; Catalini and Gans, 2020). Digital assets like cryptocurrencies and tokens are issued and transferred using blockchain technology. Anything can be stored on blockchain technology. For example, a smart contract is computer code that automatically performs predetermined actions and is stored on a blockchain. Blockchains like Ethereum, Solana, and Cardano are specifically designed to support smart contracts as a core functionality. With smart contracts, it is possible to automatically exchange a certain amount of currency for another between two counterparties when a prespecified threshold is met. Suppose the smart contract code verifies the presence of the required threshold and the currency from each counterparty. In that case, the smart contract will execute the transaction, thus eliminating the need for third parties to facilitate it.

The cost reductions brought about by blockchain and smart contracts encourage those who need to engage in a transaction to adopt blockchains as a substitute for more costly forms of intermediation typically necessary to verify that certain conditions are met. This suggests that industries with high degrees of centralization, such as finance, may benefit the most from this cost reduction. Nevertheless, there may be barriers to adoption. For example, high-fee institutional arrangements often remain entrenched even in the presence of more-efficient alternatives (Judge, 2015). Another barrier to achieving these benefits may be the hold-up problem, which occurs when multiple participants bring together valuable assets to do business, but one or more of the participants must make relationship-specific investments. Such relationship-specific investments put those who contribute early into an unfavorable negotiating position later on, which allows later participants to take advantage of the early participant (Holden and Malani, 2021). These hold-up problems are a common economic theme that emerges across financial innovations as discussed in Section 3.8.

Despite the benefits of decreases in the cost of state verification, there may be unintended consequences. Some blockchains are permissionless, meaning the validation of state is part of the computer code, so no intermediaries are necessary. Permissionless blockchains commonly use proof-of-work (PoW) or proof-of-stake (PoS) to ensure security. Both approaches have advantages and disadvantages (Budish, 2018; Cong and He, 2019; Saleh, 2020; Abadi and Brunnermeier, 2022). PoW is bad for the environment as it requires lots of energy; PoS is susceptible to large stakeholder collaboration (e.g., monopoly-like actions) or distortions brought about through intermediation chains (Azar et al., 2024) given that only a handful of validators participate in mining the blocks. Alternative consensus mechanisms, such as proof-of-authority (PoA), proof-of-access, or proof-of-personhood (PoP), have yet to achieve broad adoption.

To understand the full extent of the negative consequences potentially imposed by blockchain applications, consider the noteworthy example of Meta's attempt at launching a stablecoin (i.e., Libra/Diem). Much like the Sarbanes-Oxley Act in 2002 was a reaction to Enron, or Dodd-Frank Act in 2010 was a reaction to the financial crisis, arguably, recent regulation and proposed legislation appears to have been a direct reaction to the idea of Libra/Diem (e.g., while this study focuses on the U.S., the European Union's Markets in Crypto-Assets Act (MiCA) regulation surrounding asset-referenced tokens appears to be a direct response). Before the sale and eventual abandonment of Libra/Diem, the regulatory concern was that Meta, a company with a repository of social data covering approximately three billion people worldwide, could match that social data with transaction-level spending data. This could lead to systematic violation of privacy, exploitation of behavioral tendencies, and ultimately, a form of power that could compete with sovereigns.

Moreover, if algorithmic or fiat-based stablecoins achieved widespread adoption, this could introduce new risks to the financial system (Gorton and Zhang, 2021; Catalini et al., 2022). Some of the main concerns justifying financial regulator scrutiny are: (i) the potential for run externalities, where a rapid sell-off of one stablecoin could trigger systemic problems (e.g., similar to what occurred with Terra/Luna), and (ii) the gradual reduction in traditional bank deposits that might occur without consideration for the externality this would impose given the role these deposits play in the payments system (Bertsch, 2023). As U.S. regulators prepare stablecoin legislation, additional political and economic concerns around potential negative consequences of stablecoins are emerging, ranging from the loss of monetary policy autonomy and thereby, the inability to stabilize local business cycles, to reduced efficacy of economic sanctions, to potentially dampening feedback effects such as existing institutions catering to stablecoin issuers preferences which inadvertently reduce real economic activity.

Much of the public discourse about cryptocurrency regulation has focused on the dangers of cryptocurrencies. These risks exist, and there is a need for targeted regulation to address potential harms that flow from this. However, it is equally important not to overemphasize these risks and lose sight of the substantial benefits, economic or otherwise, that may be gained through legitimate applications of the technology. In fact, despite the potential for negative externalities, other blockchain applications beyond stablecoins are more complementary to financial services. Consider Ripple's RippleNet which transforms cross-border payments by replacing Society for Worldwide Financial Telecommunications (SWIFT)'s error-prone manual system with an instant, traceable network that reduces transaction costs and eliminates delays. Further, Ripple's on-demand liquidity feature leveraged its token (XRP) to eliminate the need for prefunded nostro/vostro accounts, freeing up capital while providing smaller financial institutions a competitive advantage in global transactions.

Another benefit of decreasing the cost of state verification via blockchain is that the cost savings can be passed to the customer. This is important for customers who face extraordinarily high fees, as the reduction in cost could be what brings them into the financial system. As with the Ripple example, tremendous costs are associated with settling international transactions. The average transaction fee for cross-border payments is around 10% and has an average clearance period of two to three days. In contrast, various blockchains enable users to transact quickly and at nearly zero cost. By dissolving the financial barriers between developed and developing nations and offering a low-cost network of frictionless international payments, blockchains have the potential to bring financial services to billions of people who would otherwise be left behind. While solutions have been created outside of the financial system, like Transferwise, blockchain-based solutions can provide cost savings even for transactions that require provenance.

Another specific benefit of blockchain is its potential to catalyze innovation because it helps solve the problem of hidden intangible value. From an accounting perspective, only patents, noncompetes, customer lists, and other intangible assets that can be tied to a specific cash flow stream are typically recorded as intangible assets on the balance sheet. Otherwise, it is only through an acquisition that the intrinsic value of an organically developed intangible asset (e.g., influential brand) converts to a market value and is assigned a value on the balance sheet. Interestingly, smart contracts can be adapted to potentially transform any transaction that requires intermediated validation, such as certifications of authenticity or future cash flows. This certification of authenticity is at the core of incentivizing content creation and/or unlocking the idle collateral value of these organically created intangible assets awaiting sale.

Finally, machine-to-machine payments enabled by blockchain-based technologies are beneficial because these micropayment systems can mitigate market distortions. Basic Attention Token (BAT) exemplifies this benefit in digital advertising, where it creates a direct value exchange between content creators, advertisers, and users based on actual attention metrics. By allowing browsers to be automatically compensated by publishers for content consumption, yet only requiring advertisers to pay for verified attention, BAT eliminates the ability of tech platforms to extract a disproportionately high share of the rents simply from enabling a match between consumers and products. This direct machine-to-machine payment system reduces fraud, improves targeting efficiency, increases equity for content creators, and restores proper price signals to a market previously distorted by opaque algorithms and centralized gatekeepers. The result is a more transparent ecosystem where resources flow according to genuine value exchange rather than platform leverage.

3.5 DeFi and DAOs

DeFi builds upon the advances brought about by blockchain. The analogy to blockchain's reduction of the cost of state verification and AI's reduction of the cost of prediction and exploration is that DeFi and DAOs reduce the need for labor-driven intermediation (e.g., underwriters or managers), concentration of power (e.g., systemically important financial institutions), and enforcement costs. DeFi protocols often run on smart contracts. DAO governance runs on smart contracts. Since smart contracts create binding, automated agreements that execute precisely as programmed without requiring trusted intermediaries, the DeFi contract's commitments reduce counterparty risk and enforcement costs. From an aspirational point of view, one could argue that DeFi and DAOs minimize the cost of building and/or coordinating complex financial and managerial services.

Yet, as we will see, DeFi and DAOs also introduce new coordination costs because a distributed structure is costly to maintain. Further, while the promise of DeFi is often presented as fully automated and trustless, human involvement remains necessary in many aspects, creating complications that challenge the ideal of pure commitments through code and reduced costs of coordinating complex activities. In particular, complications that continue to arise even in this new, supposedly more efficient setting are governance challenges in DAOs, coding errors in smart contracts, potential for manipulation when accessing external data from oracles, and the need to interact with traditional legal and regulatory systems should emergencies arise (e.g., hacking). These human elements in DeFi create a tension between the theoretical ideal of pure code-based commitments and the practical reality where human judgment, coordination, and trust are still required at various levels. This is why some critics argue that many DeFi projects are not genuinely decentralized but represent different trust and authority arrangements.

Despite these caveats, DeFi does allow parties to create precisely tailored and highly complex economic arrangements that execute via smart contracts almost instantaneously and ideally without the need for an intermediary or other trusted party. Moreover, all DeFi transactions are recorded on the ledger of a public blockchain network. Blockchains are useful not only for settling transactions but also for coordinating activity. Thus, an increasingly popular way to manifest coordination is through DAOs. Given the cost reductions and efficiencies associated with blockchains, developers can create transparent organizations, referred to as DAOs, that are less hierarchical in nature.

These DAOs use smart contracts to prevent people from stealing pooled assets or engaging in other forms of agency costs, thereby creating trust within the organization. DAOs often give people the ability to use smart contracts in voting-based systems to allow users to provide judgment or governance in a more decentralized way. In this sense, one may solve the classic agency cost problems first described in Berle and Means (1932) by creating headless organizations not run by a board or professional managers.

The products and services associated with DeFi often resemble offerings from traditional, centralized financial markets. For example, users can obtain a loan upon posting collateral, much like conventional collateralized loans. Yet DeFi takes on many additional forms, including asset trading and derivative transactions. While the earliest applications were built on blockchain-based tokens or stablecoins, recent applications incorporate real-world assets (RWAs), such as real estate, IP rights, and private credit. Similarly, the original DAO was formed in 2016 and operated much like a VC fund, by pooling assets and voting in a decentralized manner on potential investments to make profits. Ultimately, the original DAO was shut down due to a human coding error, but many new DAOs are forming, including those that have limited liability (LAOs) and larger user bases, such that they are operating similarly to a community of users with a bank account.

The key to offering DeFi products and services cheaply is the fact that they are open source, interoperable "stacks." The stacking or layering of a base blockchain with protocols, assets, and ultimately, user-facing aggregation layers, re-creates complex financial services by modularizing the input components. Moreover, since there are so many different possibilities for combining modularized components, some DeFi service providers allow users to pick and assemble a fully customized set of services. In fact, the variety of finely tailored products that can be created is extraordinary and likely to grow. Consider that there are efforts to combine predictive AI, such as those determining what financial services a user needs, with a fully customizable set of DeFi services rather than a few prepackaged offerings, such as those currently offered by robo-advisers (D'Acunto et al., 2019). AI × crypto applications, such as these, are discussed in more detail in Section 3.7.

DeFi products and services can be cheaper and more customizable, so they serve as an attractive substitute to traditional financial intermediation. In particular, boilerplate language that bankers and lawyers routinely place into transactions can be converted to code, substantially reducing the need for expensive human capital. Yet, DeFi and traditional intermediation are not perfect substitutes. In particular, relative to traditional financial services, DeFi applications incorporate new risks (Schar, 2021). In part, the risk with DeFi arises because regulatory and compliance practices differ on-chain from what happens in the traditional system. For example, there is no deposit insurance on DeFi, prices are volatile, and the whole system is subject to financial crime and cyber risk.

The novel risks associated with DeFi may resolve themselves through continuous improvement of the DeFi product, or create a segmented market if incumbents do not embrace the underlying technology in the same way they have for AI and private blockchain applications. As an example of an improvement against cyber risk, consider decentralized exchanges (DEXs), which enable direct peer-to-peer cryptocurrency trading without intermediaries, primarily using automated market makers (AMMs) instead of order books. Trading on a DEX reduces some risk because users maintain custody of their funds instead of placing them directly in a custodian's control. Yet a constant product formula ($x \times y = k$) is commonly the mathematical foundation for many DEXs like Uniswap, where x and y represent the quantities of two tokens in a liquidity pool, and k is a constant that must be maintained after every trade. This mechanism automatically adjusts prices based on supply and demand, creating a self-balancing market that operates entirely through smart contracts. While using DEXs solves for custody risk, they introduce entirely new risks like price slippage for big trades and front-running on users' pending transactions. Thus, just as with AI and other blockchain applications, we are seeing that advances in DAOs and DeFi applications eliminate certain economic inefficiencies while simultaneously creating new economic distortions. These distortions may resemble familiar problems (like front-running) or represent novel inefficiencies.

3.6 NFTs, SBTs, RWAs

NFTs represent ownership of a digital or nondigital asset and can be created on most public and private blockchains, although they are most popular on Ethereum. They differ from traditional fungible tokens because they cannot be exchanged for an identical asset. Thus, NFTs represent an innovation in digital property rights because they solve a key challenge brought about by Web2, namely, ownership and content creation verification. While the previous section outlined how blockchain generally reduces verification costs, NFTs specifically solve the double-spending problem in digital content markets. The double-spending problem in digital content markets refers to the inherent challenge that digital content, unlike physical goods, can be perfectly copied and distributed infinitely without diminishing the original. This creates a fundamental economic obstacle. If a digital asset can be replicated without cost or quality loss, establishing scarcity becomes impossible through technical means alone, undermining traditional ownership models and creators' ability to monetize their work. Put another way, prior to NFTs, digital content could be perfectly replicated at zero marginal cost, enabling widespread distribution but undermining creators' ability to capture value. This market failure led to the rise of platform intermediaries, who aggregated and monetized content, while creators often captured minimal economic rents.

NFTs resolve this tension through a novel combination of technological and economic mechanisms. By enabling verifiable scarcity in digital goods, NFTs create artificial rivalry in otherwise nonrival digital goods. Thus, while NFTs do not prevent the copying of the underlying digital content itself, they establish a cryptographically secure record of ownership for a specific token that represents the official or authentic version of that content. The immutable nature of the blockchain means that the NFT's blockchain-based record can serve as a solution to digital asset ownership. These benefits help to transform the economics of digital content markets in several fundamental ways. First, NFTs enable direct monetization of digital creation without requiring traditional intermediaries. Second, NFTs create secondary markets for digital goods, enabling price discovery and speculation. Third, NFTs enable new forms of bundling between digital ownership rights and ancillary benefits or governance privileges. Fourth, NFTs facilitate the digital–physical divide by providing a pathway forward for tokenizing unique RWAs like real estate.

NFTs have moved beyond the digital art applications popularized by Beeple, providing a useful mechanism for converting previously illiquid intangible assets into tradable financial instruments. However, research reveals significant market inefficiencies with NFTs that may extend to other assets. For example, Huang and Goetzmann (2023) document investor over-extrapolation bias and selection effects when sales increase and prices rise for NFTs. White et al. (2022) establish correlations between NFT news and subsequent returns, and Borri et al. (2022) demonstrate how rarity impacts NFT valuations. These findings parallel historical periods of financial innovation, where the novelty interacted with users' behavioral tendencies in ways that were not welfare-enhancing.

Despite these potential inefficiencies, NFTs have particular relevance for IP markets, where traditional copyright and patent systems face increasing strain from digital technologies. NFTs enable automated usage rights enforcement through smart contracts, potentially reducing monitoring and enforcement costs in IP markets. Moreover, the ability to fractionalize IP ownership through NFTs creates new possibilities for risk sharing and capital formation in creative industries. In the case of NFTs, fractionalization is often used as it allows smaller investors to pool resources to purchase fractional interests of an NFT. For example, there are platforms exclusively focused on fractional investing and enabling the purchase of truly illiquid assets like the full skeletons of dinosaurs.

However, these benefits come with some economic tradeoffs. Sockin and Xiong (2022) highlight how artificial scarcity in digital goods can create deadweight loss through reduced access. This raises questions about the optimal balance between creator incentives and social welfare in digital content markets. Additionally, the speculative nature of NFT markets, especially for art and other collectibles, can lead to bubble dynamics and coordination failures, particularly when value depends heavily on social consensus rather than fundamental utility. In particular, Oh et al. (2024) propose a framework for understanding NFTs as digital Veblen goods: consumers demand them partly because other consumers do. This makes demand for NFT collections fragile, and issuers respond by underpricing their NFTs in primary markets, creating profit opportunities for scalpers.

At the same time, there seem to be some promising applications for NFTs, especially connected to RWAs. For example, consider the benefits in the real estate context. A piece of real estate represented by an NFT allows for the transfer of ownership, which can be executed automatically via a smart contract when the NFT is sold. It is well established in finance that securitization and equitization have contributed to more efficient public markets by enabling fractional ownership, investor accessibility, and improvements in liquidity, and it appears in some instances that these benefits can be extended to a more extensive set of activities. However, these services have primarily been focused on more homogeneous assets associated with public market exchange. NFTs are helping to extend the concept of fractionalization to traditionally illiquid private markets. Thus, RWA tokenization represents a significant innovation in financial market infrastructure, enabling the representation of traditional financial assets like Treasury bonds, real estate, and private credit as digital assets on blockchain networks.

As of December 2024, the total value of tokenized RWA reached $15.3 billion in Assets Under Management (AUM), with private credit ($9.1 billion), treasuries ($4.1 billion), commodities ($1.1 billion), alternative investments, such as collectibles ($0.5 billion), institutional funds, such as opening up private equity giant KKR's Strategic Healthcare Fund through tokenization ($0.4 billion), stablecoins backed by RWA-collateral other than traditional fiat ($0.2 billion), and real estate ($0.2 billion) according to data from RWA.xyz. The RWA sector has exhibited remarkable growth, expanding from $2 billion in early 2023 to its current scale. The market's development has been driven by major institutional participants, including BlackRock's BUIDL Treasury fund and Franklin Templeton's tokenized asset initiative, suggesting a structural shift in how traditional financial institutions approach digital asset markets. This rapid institutionalization of RWA tokenization indicates the desire for tradability, accessibility, and liquidity in these traditionally illiquid, nonhomogeneous private assets.

Another innovation in tokenization from an economic perspective is SBTs, which extends the concept of a unique ownership of a digital asset to nontransferable assets such as digital credentials. As explained by Ohlhaver et al. (2022), SBTs address fundamental economic problems in identity and reputation markets. Traditional credential systems suffer from several market failures: high verification costs, limited portability, and vulnerability to falsification. SBTs potentially resolve these issues through cryptographic verification and permanent wallet association. The economic implications of SBTs are particularly relevant for labor markets, professional certification, and social cohesion. By enabling credible, portable proof of skills, experience, achievements, or social status, SBTs could reduce information asymmetries in hiring, contracting, and trust-building. Weyl et al. (2025) demonstrate how SBTs might reduce screening costs and improve match quality in social media for purposes of trust building. These ideas can also be applied to labor markets as the nontransferability of SBTs creates novel interactions with traditional models of human capital development and signaling. For example, it could lead to positive assortative matching as high-moral or high-productivity workers match with those firms with similar traits.

Next, IP law could evolve in response to easily traceable, immutable ownership records. Traditional copyright law developed around assumptions of rival, excludable physical goods and centralized enforcement mechanisms. NFTs and SBTs challenge these assumptions by enabling new forms of digital property rights that are simultaneously public (visible on blockchain) and exclusive (controlled through private keys). This creates room for the law to be modified and new ways for thinking about the interaction between on-chain and off-chain rights enforcement. The implications for copyright law are particularly complex. While NFTs can represent ownership rights, the relationship between token ownership and traditional copyright privileges remains ambiguous. Bodó et al. (2018) analyze how smart contracts might automate copyright licensing and royalty distribution, potentially reducing transaction costs in creative industries. However, this automation also raises questions about fair use, first sale doctrine, and other traditional concepts in IP law (Kappos et al., 2023). Some advocates argue this would allow one to easily track ownership and therefore, we should include a percentage of the resale back to the creator, which some platforms are experimenting with.

Looking forward, it is clear that NFTs, like other FinTech innovations, solve for one market failure while introducing new ones. Previously, there was a market failure in which creators often captured minimal economic rents because they could not establish scarcity. However, by artificially limiting access to digital goods, NFTs create deadweight loss through reduced access, where some consumers who value the good above its marginal cost but below market prices are excluded. Further, behavioral biases in NFT markets, such as investor over-extrapolation and the digital Veblen goods phenomenon, parallel conventional FinTech concerns about exploiting vulnerable populations. Finally, the ambiguous relationship between on-chain NFT ownership and traditional copyright privileges introduces new forms of coordination failure. These new economic distortions suggest that targeted regulatory approaches, such as distinguishing between consumptive and investment NFTs, clarifying IP rights, and preventing market manipulation, would enhance efficiency without stifling innovation in this emerging asset class.

3.7 AI × Crypto

While capital started to be meaningfully raised for AI × crypto projects in 2020, primarily in the data and compute space as highlighted by Cong et al. (2022), the generative AI boom of 2022 catalyzed crypto developers to embrace the intersection of the two technologies and integrate even more enthusiastically. So far, most projects can be grouped into one of four AI × crypto subcategories, including compute, data, models, and applications. Compute is the earliest and largest subcategory in this space, with multiple projects creating sizable GPU marketplaces. For example, founded in 2017, Render Network is a high-performance distributed GPU rendering network that leverages software to facilitate a compute marketplace between GPU providers (e.g., idle home computers when you are at work) and GPU requestors (e.g., major media companies like Disney and HBO, who have already signed deals with Render). The economics underlying Render are the same peer-to-peer economics driving the "sharing economy" in other areas like real estate (i.e., Airbnb) and vehicles (i.e., Uber).

The idea behind compute AI × Crypto business models is to create a two-sided marketplace for something that otherwise is not realizing its full value, such as idle compute. GPU owners monetize idle compute capacity that would otherwise go unused, creating new revenue from existing assets with minimal additional costs (i.e., mainly energy costs). This benefits creators, who are the primary target audience of Render Network, given their GPU-intensive rendering needs. Specifically, the creative users gain access to distributed GPU power without the capital expenditures of purchasing high-end hardware or committing to fixed cloud computing contracts.

Suppliers also benefit from the two-sided platform model as it can compete with centralized compute companies through lower costs, dynamic pricing, and scaling flexibility. Specifically, by tapping into underutilized GPUs, the network leverages existing hardware rather than requiring new infrastructure builds. At the same time, pricing can be dynamic and adjust based on supply and demand, potentially offering lower rates than traditional cloud rendering services, especially during periods of high supply. Relatedly, the market can naturally expand or contract based on market conditions. These features are important. The incremental compute supplier, who is being incentivized to add capacity at peak times, is much more agile than a centralized compute business, which needs to predict demand ahead of time and make large, up-front investments to build capacity.

Interestingly, like other leaders in the blockchain space (e.g., Ethereum Foundation, Solana Foundation, Stellar Foundation, Optimism Foundation, etc.), Render Network has structured itself as a Foundation but has also established a DAO to serve as a decentralized governance mechanism that enables all community members to participate by submitting and voting on Render Network proposals. This focus on allowing the community to directly influence the future development and operation of this decentralized GPU computing network stands in stark contrast to some computing networks' seemingly blackbox, authoritarian nature. These embedded governance features are more than just "vibes" as they serve a dual marketing purpose for the protocol.

The synergies between crypto and AI in the compute area are part of a larger swath of the blockchain space known as Decentralized Physical Infrastructure Networks (DePIN). The idea behind DePIN is to incentivize individuals and organizations to contribute to and manage physical infrastructure like energy grids, transportation networks, or computing power in a decentralized manner, essentially allowing anyone to participate and earn rewards for contributing resources to the network through tokens. Many business models are targeting generative AI's need for compute with their services. For instance, Aethir is a compute DePIN that connects GPU providers with enterprise clients needing high-powered chips for professional AI tasks. Helium, Akash, Storj, and Flux all offer similar business models focusing more or less on some specific niche compute areas. A broader application of DePIN is to companies like Roam, which aims to address the structural challenges facing telecoms by combining decentralized wireless infrastructure with tokenization. Through a global WiFi OpenRoaming network, Roam offers automatic, secure connectivity across millions of access points, replacing manual logins with blockchain-based authentication.

Another focus in the AI × crypto space is enabling access to high-quality data sources. As companies race to create the best frontier AI model, the total universe of human-generated data is estimated to be depleted between 2026 and 2030. While humanity will not run out of data, it is the kind of clean, well-labeled information vital for training advanced AI models that may become scarce within the next few years. In economic terms, the demand for high-quality data is rising faster than its readily available supply, creating a need for better data marketplaces and novel privacy-compatible exchange mechanisms.

Thus, similar to Render's solution in the compute space for using idle compute, efficiency gains in the data space are coming from crypto-enabled data exchanges that make use of currently siloed data. Traditional data markets often suffer from high transaction costs and lack of transparency. Blockchain-based platforms, however, can reduce these frictions. This is made possible by three key advantages: micropayment infrastructure, enhanced property rights, and reduced intermediation costs. First, crypto enables machine-to-machine transfers of value at near-zero cost. By reducing the transaction costs associated with compensating small-scale data contributions, crypto helps expand the potential data supplier market. Second, by codifying data ownership on a blockchain, data contributors receive property rights typically ignored in Web2 and, thus, can be assured of fair compensation and continued control over how their data is used. This arrangement encourages the supply of higher-quality data because contributors trust the system to reward them appropriately. Finally, several AI × crypto business models use smart contracts to reduce expenses associated with centralized control and storage of data. By eliminating the need for data infrastructure, businesses can be profitable sooner and, thereby, pass some value directly back to the data owners while still delivering data at a lower price than centralized models charge AI developers.

Data quality is also an issue that AI × crypto can help with. In response to looming data scarcity, novel business models aim to take advantage of the industry shift from "more data is better" to prioritizing high-quality data. This shift may involve synthetic, multimodal, and detailed domain-specific data or simply higher-quality, human-labeled data. Generating synthetic datasets can supplement real-world data, though there is concern about model collapse if models predominantly learn from their own generated outputs. Economically, synthetic data can reduce the dependence on rare or expensive real-world data but must be balanced against potential diminishing returns in model quality. Multi-modal data refers to information spanning multiple senses or modalities.

Commonly, this means combining text with images, audio, or video. Multimodal learning enables generative AI systems to gain a richer, more nuanced understanding by aligning information across multiple vectors.

Finally, one of the more promising areas combining AI × crypto in the data domain is using cryptographic tools to enable access to specialized data in medicine, law, engineering, and other fields. Typically, this data is too sensitive for public release but extremely valuable for the context it provides. High-quality, domain-specific data often resides behind privacy or regulatory barriers, particularly in healthcare. Cryptographic primitives such as Zero-Knowledge proofs (ZKps), Fully Homomorphic Encryption (FHE), and secure multiparty computation enable AI models to learn from private data without exposing the raw inputs. For example, some protocols help individuals tokenize their biometric data and then lease this information through smart contracts to companies. From an economic perspective, these technologies reduce risk and liability for data holders, lowering sharing costs and increasing overall supply.

These decentralized data solutions are made possible by blockchain-enabled machine-to-machine micropayment systems that when combined with smart contracts streamline compensation for data owners, making it viable to supply and purchase high-quality data contributions of any size. Because blockchain transparency enables participants to price data quality more accurately, resources flow more efficiently to the high-quality data that yields the greatest marginal improvement in frontier AI models. Finally, by reducing privacy risks, more data contributors, ranging from large institutions to individual end-users, are willing to participate in tokenized data markets.

As an example, consider Grass, a powerful data-generation engine. Imagine you want to build a vast, real-time database of virtually everything online, from product prices to job listings to social media updates. You could run your job through a single service provider and use big server farms, or you could tap into millions of ordinary people's devices worldwide. The latter is essentially what Grass does. When a firm or researcher needs to collect online data, they submit their requests to Grass's network. Grass then routes these tasks to participating user devices (Grass nodes), which retrieve the data from target websites as though the users themselves were browsing. The participating user devices (idle computers at home) receive micropayments in cryptocurrency for their service. The multimodal data retrieved from the nodes is then cleaned and structured by Grass. Effectively, Grass serves as a centralized coordinator, relying on validators and routers to ensure data quality and provenance. By harnessing millions of contributors worldwide, Grass can efficiently gather large volumes of publicly available web information on a daily basis. This decentralized model also reduces blind spots in the data gathering process as it gets around the barriers that traditional web crawlers encounter (time-outs, request limits), and therefore, Grass can provide higher-quality data.

Turning from data and compute, the third subcategory of AI × crypto is AI models. AI models are trained systems that can perform predictions based on input data, whether predicting the next word in a sentence, as in the case of LLMs, or predicting the best trade for an investor's portfolio. Notably, the parameters that define frontier AI models are typically chosen by humans, introducing a way for bias to leak into the system. For instance, data labeling, feature selection, imbalance in class representation, postprocessing on model outputs, and hyperparameter tuning all influence a model's performance. Importantly, even narrow finetuning such as on a small amount of insecure code or even inaccurate numbers can produce broadly misaligned LLMs on almost everything else they output such as offering misinformation (Betley et al., 2025).

Like centralized entities seeking to achieve AGI, DGI is a primary goal of the business models in this space. DGI is the notion that an AI system, rather than running as one monolithic model in a single data center, could operate across many different machines or nodes (potentially owned by different people or organizations). The hope is that by distributing data, computation, and decision-making power, the model has greater resilience, less influence from any single controlling entity, and the potential to scale in ways traditional centralized systems cannot.

In practice, current large-centralized AGI efforts from OpenAI to Google's DeepMind and others have the lead. Nevertheless, the promise of DGI remains an attractive investment to some as it is one of the only ways to combat centralized control of powerful frontier AI models. For example, Sentient Technologies, which is often associated with Peter Thiel, is experimenting with a decentralized approach to AI models. It focuses on e-commerce AI models and spreading computational tasks across a large, distributed infrastructure. This approach of focusing on a specific problem is more common at the intersection of AI × crypto.

For example, Numerai is a hedge fund that crowdsources AI models from data scientists worldwide. It does so by supplying high-quality, anonymized financial data for free. In return, data scientists compete to develop predictive AI models, staking Numerai's token on their models. If their models perform well, they earn rewards in proportion to how much Numerai uses their model. As a second example, Bittensor is a decentralized protocol that rewards developers for creating and sharing AI models. Like Numerai, Bittensor uses token-based incentives to encourage high-quality model contributions. However, the two differ in both purpose and structure. Bittensor aims to build a global marketplace for AI services, in which model creators earn tokens as payment for others using (or benefiting from) their models. Thus, Bittensor is one of the few projects attempting to combine blockchain incentives with an open, general AI framework. Developers retain more control, and an open network can potentially aggregate thousands of specialized models to create a competitive model with AGI. Thus, Bittensor's approach counters centralized AGI models by incentivizing a global community to share and refine models openly.

The final category of AI × crypto is applications, which include AI agents and authentication services. This area is growing fast because, whether or not DGI is achieved, blockchain developers can integrate frontier centralized AI models into applications. An AI model, for instance, could be implemented into a DeFi-style application to rebalance a portfolio optimally. As some proponents argue, adding these AI models to blockchains makes the most sense since blockchains provide a deterministic, transparent, and tamper-resistant platform where smart contracts already function much like simple autonomous agents. Extending this idea, some believe that more advanced AI agents, which are capable of making decisions, owning digital assets, and interacting with external data via oracles, could naturally live on-chain. Because blockchains enforce contract rules programmatically and are difficult to shut down or censor, agentic AI running on them could, in theory, operate with minimal human intervention.

In practice, AI agents can be constructed to self-reflect, use tools, plan, and collaborate with other agents, allowing them to mimic traditional workflow loops more closely. From an economic perspective, agentic AI offers specialization, which is helpful in the workplace. Specifically, AI agents can be programmed to concentrate on a specific function, leading to greater efficiency, high-quality outputs, and continuous improvement through repeated practice. By excelling at narrow tasks, agentic AI systems can be aggregated to tackle complex problems in a highly coordinated and efficient manner. In this sense, agentic AI brings the composability that blockchain is famous for offering customers in a setting previously dominated by broad, one-size-fits-all automation. They hold meaningful promise because specialized AI agents can be created and modified more rapidly, adapt to new tasks more flexibly, and continuously refine their skills.

When these agentic AI systems operate on a blockchain, they benefit from a transparent and tamper-resistant infrastructure that enables seamless collaboration. The blockchain provides a reliable ledger of contributions, ensuring each specialized agent's work is recorded and verified without centralized oversight. It also automates incentives: agents can be rewarded in proportion to their contributions, encouraging participants to develop ever more specialized and effective models. This self-reinforcing loop, where each agent gains feedback, improves its function, and is compensated for its utility, leads to a more dynamic and innovative environment. It is also the case that all of these agents are "unbanked" and the traditional financial system is unlikely to want to onboard these agents, leaving crypto as their primary avenue to both make and receive payments.[3]

Thus, it's worthwhile to think through a concrete example. Imagine a decentralized entity with a chatbot interface run by various AI agents. The chatbot could build a following by posting appealing content to social media and generating income in multiple ways from its audience. It could manage and invest those earnings through cryptocurrencies. It is quite feasible that such an entity could become a fully autonomous billion-dollar entity in time. In later sections, we will consider the gaps regulators face in serving these DAEs, but for now, it is worth recognizing that there are already examples of this, ranging from Truth Terminal, which gained popularity on X, to robots like Gaka-chu, which makes a living as an entrepreneurial painter and manages its' earnings through cryptocurrencies (Ferrer et al., 2023). In fact, many blockchain analysts are predicting a dramatic increase in the role of AI agents in the ecosystem. VanEck predicts one million AI agents on the blockchain by the end of 2025, and others argue that Web3 agents will be blockchain's leading creators and consumers.

Finally, AI has made creating and spreading misinformation like deceptive deep fakes cheaper. With lower barriers for malicious actors who want to circulate false content, this, in turn, has increased demand for verifying the accuracy and origins of what users encounter online. In this environment, crypto-based protocols offer a unique way to authenticate data. They do this by providing an on-chain proof of the source, effectively allowing anyone to confirm that a piece of information actually came from a specific user or AI system.

From an economic standpoint, authentication services rely on supply and demand in a new market for verifiable data. On the demand side, users, businesses, and organizations want a trusted method to ensure the information they receive is legitimate. This demand will likely grow as more deepfakes and misleading content appear, making reliable verification more important. On the supply side, crypto projects are developing decentralized protocols that allow anyone to register or prove the authenticity of data. By tokenizing these services, they create financial incentives through token rewards for participants to maintain the system's integrity.

---

[3] Some centralized AI agents, including OpenAI's Operator, can execute payments when users provide credit card credentials, but they cannot receive incoming payments or independently establish financial accounts.

Several examples illustrate both the promise and the challenges of these authentication services. Worldcoin, from OpenAI cofounder Sam Altman, focuses on proving that a user is a real person through an approach called "Proof-of-Personhood." As a second example, consider Numbers Protocol, which aims to label AI-generated content and register digital media files onchain. The main economic driver is whether enough people need reliable data verification and whether these platforms can meet that need in a scalable way. Suppose users find the solution superior to traditional verification methods, like centralized IDs or manual verification. In that case, they may be willing to pay for, stake, or support the tokens that power these authentications.

3.8 Common Economic Forces

The breadth of recent financial innovations is unusual in its expansiveness, encompassing advancements in conventional FinTech, AI, blockchain, cryptocurrencies, smart contracts, and even integrating across dimensions to create novel financial capabilities within the AI × crypto space. Before describing the regulatory responses to this wave of innovation, I examine the economic forces that underlie these innovations. In doing so, it becomes clear that driving forces often push in different directions, creating new risks and tensions. For example, have the improvements in transparency brought about by blockchain meaningfully mitigated information asymmetry, or have they introduced new distortions and complexities? Similarly, have the novel governance structures associated with decentralized organizations reduced agency costs, or do they persist and manifest in other ways?

By analyzing the extent to which recent financial innovations have brought about changes in fundamental economic phenomena, including agency costs, information asymmetry, moral hazard, hold-up problems, and coordination challenges, this subsection helps identify the new and old channels through which economic distortions may arise. These five common economic forces provide a foundational reference for subsequent sections examining regulatory and policy responses. Thus, it is necessary to have an eye toward potential solutions for mitigating such distortions and enforcing accountability for bad actors in the FinTech space.

3.8.1 Agency Costs

While many FinTech innovations have introduced greater transparency and novel incentive mechanisms into financial services, they have not eradicated agency costs. Instead, the evolving structure of financial intermediation has sometimes given rise to new agency conflicts, while other, more traditional challenges associated with agency costs, like reduced effort, remain. Corporations are a classic setting where agency costs arise, and misaligned incentives between shareholders and managers are ubiquitous. In response, a cottage industry of lawyers and consultants helps design optimal executive compensation contracts and employee stock-option plans. The nuances included in these contracts are thought to help remedy agency costs and realign managers' incentives to match shareholders. Nevertheless, most empirical estimates suggest we are far from first-best in a corporate setting.

Can DAOs overcome the challenges of agency costs? Unfortunately, agency costs persist in most decentralized settings despite governance structures being more nimble and contracting solutions being more flexible. Specifically, agency costs emerge when principals' objectives (e.g., token holders and protocol founders) diverge from agents' goals (e.g., project teams and protocol users). Unlike conventional financial systems, where regulatory oversight, legal contracts, and corporate governance practices help mitigate opportunistic behavior or eliminate shirking, DAOs use alternative governance structures powered by smart contracts. These alternative governance structures share some similarities with corporate structures in that some are set up more democratically, and some are more dictatorial (Gompers et al., 2003) but introduce new features reflective of their decentralized production process.

Appel and Grennan (2024) evaluate twenty-eight governance features commonly used by DAOs, including inclusive governance features (e.g., offering off-chain gasless voting, vote delegation capabilities, and proof-of-attendance badges for reputational benefits), security features (e.g., multiple signature requirements, feasibility studies, implementation delays), and restrictive governance features (e.g., proposal requirements, quorum thresholds, and supermajority voting). While some of these features are familiar, others, such as multiple signature requirements or time delays, are new. These new features, however, tend to focus on fostering broad participation in decision-making and mitigating malicious behavior rather than directly addressing agency costs.

For example, DAO governance often fails to incorporate classic executive contracting features (e.g., clawbacks). The decentralized nature of DAOs means they typically lack centralized leadership like CEOs, with decision-making authority instead distributed among tokenholders through voting systems. This creates unique challenges, subjecting DAOs to potential "governance attacks" where majority tokenholders can expropriate from the minority. While some DAOs implement security measures to combat this, most DAOs lack robust accountability mechanisms common in traditional corporate governance structures, such as compensation alignment structures and clear compliance frameworks.

Furthermore, DAOs, in their desire not to have their governance token classified as a security, frequently eschew traditional fiduciary duties that, at least in the corporate context, have helped facilitate efficiency. For example, the Department of Labor issued the Avon Letter in 1988 in response to free-riding and low voter turnout observations at corporations' annual meetings (Grennan and Michaely, 2025). The Avon Letter clarified that fund managers must vote on behalf of the shares they manage at annual meetings as part of their fiduciary duties. Instead, in DAOs, there is low voter participation because there is no regulatory clarity on fiduciary duty. This has led to high voting concentration among founders and venture capitalists who vote under the assumption that they have a fiduciary duty to their underlying investors.

Appel and Grennan (2023) empirically analyze over 10,000 governance proposals across 151 DAOs and show decision-making is highly centralized based on Herfindahl-Hirschman index (HHI) of voting power across top voting addresses. For the top three voting addresses, power is typically around 67 percent and these top three voters cast the majority of votes for most proposals. Further evidence of centralization is that the top three token holders tend to vote in unison. This concentration directly contradicts the decentralization ethos of DAOs and creates new agency problems where a small minority effectively controls governance decisions, potentially at the expense of other token holders. While the concentration appears to be decreasing over time (with HHI falling by 33% over the three-year sample period), the empirical evidence clearly shows that DAOs have not achieved the democratized decision-making they aspire to create. More recent evidence from Cong et al. (2025) also indicates concentrated voting in DAOs. This concentration of voting power parallels work on gerrymandering, where Friedman and Holden (2008) offer a "pack and crack" model to demonstrate how strategic actors can manipulate district boundaries to maximize control while minimizing the appearance of domination. While not systematically documented for DAOs, there are anecdotes of sophisticated tokenholders deploying voting rights across multiple wallets to create an illusion of decentralization while maintaining coordinated control.

To overcome these new variants of agency costs and free-riding introduced by decentralized governance structures, many DAOs are now experimenting with alternatives. This continued innovation and evolution will hopefully reduce the novel agency costs of early iterations of DAO governance, like those created by Compound's Governor Bravo. For example, one solution is lazy consensus, which is achieved by stating your intent to make some change on a public forum or equivalent setting and waiting a predetermined amount of time (e.g., three days) for anyone to object and, if they don't, proceed.

Another solution is representative democracy and the idea of DAO delegation (Bongaerts et al., 2025). Finally, other DAOs are pursuing a type of democracy previously only theorized about (Hart et al., 2024), whereby a set of random DAO members or a set of DAO members based on their expertise are pushed a notification on their phone and given information to vote. This randomization process with notification allows the DAO to avoid voter fatigue while maintaining a representative, democratic voice. It also allows the DAO to be adaptable to change.

Thus, a potentially more optimistic interpretation of the agency problems underlying DAOs is that they persist in the first iteration of the development process, but through continuous evolution, DAOs are modifying their governance process to match the production process they are engaged in. These modifications reduce agency costs similarly to contracting solutions for corporations, but, in this instance, they are better matched to the DAO production process. It is also worth noting that some projects and protocols are winding down their DAOs as they believe a foundation is a better legal structure for pursuing their work. Through this DAO death process, participants also learn how to reduce economic inefficiencies.

Finally, one particularly salient example of inefficiencies brought about by agency costs that still needs to be solved for the Web3 space is the market for "corporate control" (Manne, 1965). For corporations, this disciplinary force is one of the most effective ways to mitigate agency costs among managers. Yet the large degree of experimentation in DAO governance structures leads to incompatible governance systems. This is making integration costs associated with merger activity higher, nullifying this classic disciplinary force of "control" and resulting in fewer deals and weaker disciplinary incentives on the leaders of decentralized protocols (Tan et al., 2025). As experimentation continues and best practices emerge, it seems clear that an external force, whether regulatory or private (i.e., a decentralized activist hedge fund), could help reduce agency costs even further in DAOs.

Another noteworthy and related area is formalized adjudication or arbitration mechanisms for smart contract or Web3 disputes. Few blockchain-based, fully decentralized court systems exist. Aragon introduced one, but it ultimately was shut down. More recently, Kleros has emerged as a decentralized arbitration service for disputes that uses a peer-to-peer jury mechanism. Regardless of what solution or set of solutions emerges, for agency problems to be reduced, it is clear that some enforcement mechanism needs to be available for disputes. Given that the exact jurisdiction for some of these issues is debatable, having blockchain-based solutions seems inevitable unless regulators can develop some RegTech solution (see Section 5 for more on RegTech).

Finally, it is worth noting that novel or persistent agency costs are not limited to the blockchain space. Similar challenges emerge in traditional FinTech as well. Consider AI-powered credit underwriting. AI developers are tasked with creating models that optimize lending decisions, but their incentives often diverge from the lenders' long-term interests. Yet developers may be rewarded based on model adoption metrics or initial performance indicators rather than sustained loan performance over complete credit cycles. This misalignment incentivizes developers to design models that maximize approval rates for seemingly creditworthy borrowers by incorporating novel alternative data sources while potentially underweighting traditional risk factors that manifest only during economic downturns.

When economic conditions deteriorate, these models may experience unexpected degradation in performance as their training data predominantly captured behavior during favorable economic periods. The lender bears the ultimate credit risk, while the developer has already captured their compensation. This dynamic is particularly problematic in marketplace lending platforms where the developers of the scoring algorithm may have different economic interests than the capital providers funding the loans. The technical complexity of the models provides convenient cover for this misalignment, as it becomes difficult for the principals to distinguish between genuine innovation and model designs that shift risks into blind spots.

3.8.2 Information Asymmetry and Moral Hazard

Another common economic phenomenon that leads to regulatory intervention is information asymmetry. In financial markets, when one party possesses superior information relative to another, it creates the potential for adverse selection or moral hazard. This imbalance fundamentally distorts market efficiency as informed participants can exploit their informational advantage strategically. In cryptocurrency markets, information asymmetry manifests prominently in stablecoin operations where issuers claim off-chain reserves that token holders cannot completely verify. For example, investigative journalism published in the Wall Street Journal revealed that Tether used some of the interest payments from the Treasuries serving as collateral for its stablecoin (USDT) to invest in AI and neurotech startups at substantial losses (Foldy and Ostroff, 2024).

Blockchain projects purporting to do one thing (e.g., provide bank-like safety as in the case of Celsius) and doing something far different is all too common. Despite blockchain technology being immutable and transparent, the quality and composition of the collateral backing a particular token or the precise location of the wallet one transacts with (e.g., if one wants to avoid economic transactions with North Korea) are often unknown. This introduces significant counterparty risk to stablecoin holders. The prevalence of these types of situations where one party has an informational advantage and evidence of insiders' front-running downturns at Terra Luna and Celsius (Liu et al., 2023; Appel et al., 2025) suggest that a key area for regulatory clarity will be in ensuring the reliability and stability of stablecoins reserves as well as the ability to securely verify the credentials of the wallet one is transacting with. Fortunately, zero-knowledge proofs and other RegTech innovations such as portable KYC make this possible. These solutions, however, have not been mandated and as such are not being adopted en masse.

Information asymmetry also leads to challenges in DAOs. For example, principal-agent problems that lead to one party having superior information before a transaction can introduce issues like adverse selection. For example, when core developers possess technical expertise that average community members lack. Off-chain coordination among technically sophisticated participants can lead to governance proposals that appear beneficial to the broader community but disproportionately benefit insiders (Appel and Grennan, 2023; Cong et al., 2025). It is undoubtedly the case that some protocol upgrades are framed as technical improvements while subtly altering economic mechanisms to favor large stakeholders. The challenges are particularly acute because understanding the full implications of code changes requires specialized knowledge that most token holders do not possess, creating a new form of technical capture that traditional disclosure systems cannot mitigate. Therefore, grasping these novel informational distortions is important, as they may require new solutions like the unbundling of risk management services from a DeFi protocol to ensure a competitive market properly prices risk associated with technical improvements. To date, most DAOs have members or subDAOs handle such features, but a system akin to what we have with auditors and Big 4 Accounting firms may be better and ensuring stability of the whole system and greater market transparency. Here, there has been some movement in this direction with popular DeFi protocols outsourcing their services to providers like Gauntlet.

Similarly, in algorithmic trading and AI-driven portfolio management, information asymmetry can lead to economic distortions when model developers create sophisticated "black box" systems that investors cannot effectively scrutinize. The opacity of complex ML models creates information asymmetry, where developers may optimize for short-term performance metrics that attract capital rather than long-term investor value. An AI system might be trained to generate impressive short-term returns by taking on hidden risks, while marketing materials emphasize only favorable performance statistics. When retail investors have access to such advanced algorithms without having the technical expertise to evaluate them, this creates a potential moral hazard.

In the case of robo-advisors, it is undoubtedly the case that risk-shifting can occur through the introduction of hidden algorithms that favor certain products with which the robo-advisor has a partnership. Alternatively, developers using LLMs may face a moral hazard when deploying financial advisory models that generate confident-sounding recommendations with limited accountability for negative outcomes, as the attribution of causality becomes difficult when advice passes through multiple systems. Such situations are very challenging to regulate, thus necessitating potentially a multipronged system that helps realign developers' incentives with the underlying agent and out-of-the-box solutions that may involve model evaluation and certification. For example, it should be possible to stress-test or perturb an algorithmic model in various ways and not see an unfair competitive advantage to the underlying company or developer. Moreover, the temporal disconnect between when AI systems are deployed and when their failure modes become apparent creates a structural moral hazard problem, as developers can capture economic benefits before the full risk implications materialize. This suggests that regulatory frameworks must establish clear liability standards for algorithmic decision-making.

Either way, the combination of AI and blockchain creates incentives for developers to take excessive risks or commit negligence. It is also clear that the sheer number of shenanigans is much higher because of the composability of blockchain. Each piece could intertwine in a way to distort incentives further. For example, DeFi protocols may offer undercollateralized lending. Yet this choice creates an incentive for borrowers to default strategically during market downturns. Yet, leveraged yield farming platforms also exist, encouraging users to build precarious positions that can trigger cascading liquidations across the entire ecosystem. Is the solution to ban undercollateralized lending outright? Or does it serve as a building block to something else, and how can regulators best weigh the gains from these new features being readily available, with the fact that others will likely use it in ways that create fragility for the whole system? These are all situations that future regulation should consider carefully.

3.8.3 Hold-up Problems

Another common economic phenomenon is the hold-up problem, which occurs when one party makes relationship-specific investments that lose value outside the relationship. In such situations, the counterparty can exploit the vulnerability of the investing party by demanding more favorable terms based on a credible threat to walk away after the investment is made. This opportunistic renegotiation is possible because the investing party has limited outside options once committed to the relationship-specific investment. In a corporate setting, asset-specific investments between manufacturers and suppliers often create hold-up problems where specialized equipment, facilities, or systems are developed for specific counterparties. In the case of AI, some of these classic hold-up problems are occurring. In a financial intermediation setting, hold-up might occur when a borrower shares proprietary information, only to face exploitation when the lender opportunistically increases the interest rate or modifies renewal terms. Another common example is when small businesses customize their operations to meet specific requirements of payment processors or advertisers, but face potentially dramatic shifts in revenue if changes are invoked because they have become dependent on these services. This is happening with generative AI providing enough content from websites based on Google search without actually forcing clicks, thereby generating significantly lower advertisement revenue for small businesses.

In some cases, FinTech innovations were motivated by hold-up frictions, and therefore, adopting these innovations partially addresses these traditional hold-up problems through increased competition once a relational investment is made and/or through reduced switching costs. For example, marketplace lending platforms have expanded access to diverse funding sources, reducing borrower dependence on individual lenders. Data portability standards, which have become more common during the FinTech era, reduce the friction of moving between financial service providers, enabling customers to transfer their financial histories and verify their credentials faster and cheaper. Furthermore, on the corporate and industrial side, APIs and modular financial infrastructure are allowing small businesses to more easily integrate and later disengage from specific service providers without complete operational overhauls. This is only expected to increase now that Stripe, one of the largest payment services platforms for small businesses in the U.S., agreed to acquire Bridge in a $1.1-billion deal to enable their customers to accept stablecoin payments (McCurdy, 2024).

However, FinTech has not fully resolved hold-up problems and, in some cases, has merely transformed them. Many digital financial platforms still create significant switching costs through proprietary data formats, unique integration requirements, and network effects that lock users into specific ecosystems. The benefits of personalization and tailored services often come with the trade-off of increased relationship specificity, as AI-powered financial services learn user preferences and behaviors over time, creating data dependencies that cannot be easily transferred to competing platforms despite data portability rights.

FinTech innovations have also introduced novel hold-up problems. First, DeFi protocols create a form of technological hold-up when users commit significant assets to platforms that require protocol upgrades over time. Once large sums are locked in smart contracts, users become vulnerable to governance decisions by protocol developers and large token holders who can modify terms, fee structures, or risk parameters. While there are typically exit strategies, these usually come at high costs. The high costs of coordinated exit during contentious upgrades have created such meaningful leverage for insiders that it spurred the creation of the first decentralized activist hedge fund (Chaparro, 2018).

Holden and Malani (2021) provide insights into when hold-up problems will and will not be most acute with smart contracts. Unlike traditional contracts where enforceability depends on courts' willingness to grant specific performance, blockchain-encoded agreements execute automatically when verifiable conditions are met. However, there is a critical limitation, namely, that smart contracts cannot resolve hold-up problems arising from noncontractible investments or subjective performance metrics. This nuanced understanding helps explain why certain DeFi applications successfully mitigate hold-up problems (e.g., simple token swaps), while others remain vulnerable to opportunistic behavior (e.g., decisions requiring qualitative judgments). A key implication from their research is that RegTech solutions should focus on creating verifiable quality metrics that expand the range of smart contract applications capable of resolving hold-up problems. In Section 5.4, RegTech solutions are discussed in more detail.

In the AI setting, the hold-up problem might appear in several ways. First, AI training data relationships are vulnerable to relationship-specific investments and exploitation. Companies that invest heavily in collecting data for AI training may face a hold-up from AI developers who become dependent on their data. This is also true for specialized AI infrastructure. Finally, AI safety investments appear to reflect hold-up challenges. The AI safety measures that companies desire are often bespoke. If an AI service provider creates a bespoke investment, and the counterparty decides it does not need it or says it will walk away, the AI company would be out of luck. This scenario demonstrates how the threat of hold-up can lead to socially suboptimal outcomes where potentially valuable safety innovations are not developed or implemented due to concerns about future opportunistic behavior by counterparties who might exploit relationship-specific investments.

3.8.4 Coordination Failures

Coordination failures and network externalities occur when multiple parties would benefit from cooperation, but individual incentives lead them to act otherwise, resulting in suboptimal collective outcomes despite potential gains from coordinated action. These market failures are particularly pronounced in systems that derive value from widespread adoption and interoperability, where fragmentation can significantly diminish utility for all participants. In traditional financial markets, coordination failures manifest through liquidity fragmentation across trading venues, incompatible payment systems across jurisdictions, and competing technical standards that impede efficiency. These challenges often require regulatory intervention or industry consortia to establish common protocols that overcome individual actors' short-term incentives to differentiate or capture market share through proprietary solutions.

The intersection of AI and cryptocurrency technologies faces substantial coordination challenges that could impede their development. Decentralized compute networks for AI training and inference risk fork wars as competing governance philosophies or economic models emerge, potentially splitting computational resources and fragmenting the liquidity of associated tokens. Cross-chain incompatibility presents another significant hurdle, as AI models and agents operating across different blockchain ecosystems struggle with inconsistent data standards, security assumptions, and settlement mechanisms. Oracle systems that feed external data to AI-powered smart contracts remain vulnerable to manipulation and exploits, particularly when economic incentives for honest reporting weaken during periods of market stress or when adversarial actors can profit from temporary misinformation. Similarly, AI agent coordination problems may arise where individually rational behavior leads to collective inefficiencies, such as computational resource congestion or strategic withholding of capabilities that would benefit the broader ecosystem.

While the cryptocurrency ecosystem demonstrated remarkable resilience during the Silicon Valley Bank crisis by containing potential systemic contagion, smaller-scale coordination failures continue to hamper technological progress and adoption. Localized inefficiencies like competing technical standards or fragmented liquidity across too many similar protocols that cannot consolidate suggest that coordination challenges remain a significant obstacle. One promising area is AI × Crypto, where the AI may be able to help navigate these coordination failures, making it a substantial but not insurmountable hurdle. In this sense, unlike purely technical problems solved with engineering, coordination challenges typically require institutional innovations that align incentives across diverse stakeholders. Allowing AI agents armed with a bank account to act on our behalf may finally solve some of these challenges. Of course, to ensure this happens, mitigating the challenges posed by other economic phenomena like agency costs and information asymmetries is essential. It is also the case that developing better decentralized governance standards and interoperability standards would go a long way toward determining whether FinTechs can deliver on their promise of more efficient, transparent financial systems or remain constrained by different shades of the same economic phenomena they were brought in to solve.

3.9 What Areas of Financial Services Are Technology Resistant?

It is worth noting that while emerging financial technologies can replicate and expand the current offerings of financial services firms like banks, insurance companies, and asset management firms, there are still areas of financial services in which emerging technologies are mostly absent. Consider investment banking, which includes underwriting for debt and equity issuances, and advising companies involved in mergers and acquisitions. These deals are still driven by human capital, client experience, reputation, and excellence in execution. The industry is comprised of many small, boutique investment banks that specialize in providing bespoke, artisan-like services to their clients. These complex tasks still appear to be technology resistant, although some aspects of the overall service are being offered more efficiently (e.g, investment banking analysts can save time using generative AI to help write first drafts of pitchbooks). Finally, while some AI and alternative data providers are helping in the due diligence process for M&A deals, there is not a decentralized application for sourcing M&A deals or getting clients through negotiations and regulatory review. Similarly, while token sales or DeFi loans may represent an alternative way for startups to raise capital to fund their business, the underwriting quality and size of the underwriters' networks still matter for these offerings. Thus, it is more common for applications to focus on the tools such as providing an AI chatbot that offer investors and traders answers to bond-related covenant questions rather than underwriting and placing the bond specifically. Nevertheless, some in the crypto space are making use of rights granted to investment circles and similar smaller entities to explore the potential of fully autonomous underwriting processes.

4 The Regulation of FinTech (Present)

4.1 AI

In the case of AI, a prominent failure meriting regulatory intervention is that algorithms can be biased (Bartlett et al., 2022). Such bias causes harm, especially when the systems are deployed too hastily (e.g., audits of face recognition systems repeatedly show racial and gender bias; audits of credit screens show that they are biased). Other market failures relate to manipulation that targets vulnerable populations (e.g., realistic deep-fakes that vulnerable populations do not realize are AI-embedded). There are also, of course, externalities, such as the climate impact of energy-guzzling deep learning models, and the potential displacement of high-skilled workers.

4.1.1 Federal initiatives

Early on, U.S. regulation for AI was fragmented and involved sector-specific policy guidance, pilot studies, voluntary frameworks for compliance, formal standards, or other policy vehicles and related guidelines. Given that a sector-specific approach required the identification of the appropriate statutory authority, which may or may not be sympathetic to emerging technologies, innovators complained about regulatory policy uncertainty. For example, self-driving cars are regulated by the Department of Transportation (DoT), while AI for health is overseen by the Food and Drug Administration (FDA). Therefore, technology specialists advocated for a cross-industry approach toward AI regulation related to AI specific issues in order to provide more consistency. Ultimately, numerous provisions of consequence across industries for AI are being implemented via national defense policy rather than banking or securities regulations. Given that the stakes are higher for optimizing AI policy in the context of defense (life and death) than finance (richer or poorer) or advertising (relevant or not), the approach may provide some insights into how policy for blockchain and DeFi applications could move forward.

In January 2021, the Defense Authorization Act was approved by the U.S. Congress. The Act includes several provisions related to AI such as the creation of a new National AI Initiative Office led by the White House. The National AI Initiative Office's mission is to serve as the point of contact for federal AI activities for federal departments and agencies, as well as other public and private entities that may be involved in the initiative. In particular, an interagency committee is tasked with providing coordination of federal AI research and development (R&D) activities as well as education and workforce training activities across the government. The committee will have rotating representatives from the Department of Commerce, the National Science Foundation (NSF), and the Department of Energy (DoE). Other key provisions include the Department of Defense (DoD) and the Commerce Department's National Institute of Standards and Technology (NIST) being tasked with advancing collaborative frameworks on AI, as well as new technical standards and guidelines that mitigate risk and promote trustworthiness. A key pillar toward achieving trustworthy AI is the establishment of common definitions such as AI explainability, transparency, safety, and privacy. A key goal is to provide case studies of successful AI framework implementation and help businesses and researchers align with international standards in the coming years.

4.1.2 Enforcement Actions

Enforcement is another important component of incentivizing innovation and the implementation of unbiased AI-powered algorithms in finance. The SEC has brought several recent cases that help clarify "best practices" with regard to AI and big data. Many firms collect data, including from equity market intelligence firms primarily focused on the financial industry, as well as firms that are commercializing consumer products. In 2021, the SEC sent a cease-and-desist letter to AppAnnie, which is a seller of market data on how apps on mobile devices are performing, including data on the number of times a particular company's app is downloaded, the amount of revenue that a company is generating through its app, and how often customers are using that company's app. The SEC alleges that AppAnnie violated the antifraud provisions of the federal securities laws by making material misrepresentations about how AppAnnie's alternative data was derived and what powered its proprietary AI algorithm.

In particular, AppAnnie's terms of use assured app creators that opted into AppAnnie's services that it would only use anonymized data and that no material nonpublic information would be provided to AppAnnie's customers whether they were hedge funds or industry competitors. In practice, AppAnnie's data science team took user metrics obtained from app creators but not intended for use in proprietary algorithms to build the model. The model was then sold to hedge funds, so the SEC built a case against AppAnnie for violating the securities laws by engaging in "manipulative and deceptive devices in connection with the purchase or sale of a security." In their settlement, AppAnnie agreed to completely disregard the AI model built with the inappropriate data. A plausible alternative would have been to keep using the model but replace the inappropriate data with appropriate data. Given that this alternative did not occur, it suggests that future enforcement actions by the SEC may follow the same logic. That is, what was created with illegally used data (e.g., an AI model or product) is also tainted. This parallels fruit of the poisonous tree doctrine used to determine when evidence is admissible in court (Frankfurter, 1939). For FinTech developers, this suggests that if the data is tainted, so is the product.

The SEC has other ways to police lax data handling as well, including Regulation S-P, which requires registered brokers, dealers, investment companies, and investment advisers have written policies to safeguard the financial and personal information of consumers. Other government entities have similar requirements, including, but not limited to, the New York State Department of Financial Services and Commonwealth of Massachusetts Securities Division.

Finally, another relevant case involves SoFi favoring its own products in its algorithm. The SEC recently settled with robo-adviser SoFi Wealth for breaching its fiduciary duties to clients in connection with its April 2019 investment of client assets into two new exchange-traded funds (ETFs) sponsored by its parent company, Social Finance, Inc. (SoFi). Many robo-advisers are seeking organic growth opportunities through cross-selling opportunities. These conflicts present many difficult questions: Is it sufficient for robo-advisers to simply disclose that they favor their own proprietary investments? What if those proprietary investments underperform? Alternatively, what if those ETFs cost more or have high associated fees? Further, the financial advisory business is notorious for misconduct (Egan et al., 2019): does the removal of the friend/person layer cause more damage? In automating the project, are they disclosing to clients the full extent of the risk associated with their investments?

Specifically, SoFi Wealth sold the third-party ETFs its clients held and used the proceeds from those sales to purchase positions in the SoFi ETFs, which in turn triggered tax consequences for many of SoFi Wealth's clients. The SEC order finds that, prior to the execution of these transactions, SoFi Wealth had failed to disclose to clients conflicts of interest associated with the transactions. Specifically, the SEC order finds that SoFi Wealth's disclosures did not explain that SoFi Wealth (1) preferred SoFi's proprietary ETFs over third-party ETFs as investment options for clients, and that SoFi's economic interest in these proprietary ETFs presented a conflict of interest for SoFi Wealth, (2) invested client assets in these proprietary ETFs to help market the SoFi brand as having a broader array of services and products than previously offered, or (3) intended to use client assets to capitalize the new SoFi ETFs with significant investment on their second day of trading, making the SoFi ETFs more liquid and favorable to the market.

Given that securities markets require an understanding of the economic incentives of the various actors to understand the effects of the regulatory regime and the efforts of the regime. For typical securities, anti-fraud liability lends credibility to a firm's disclosures, so high value firms will want to disclose to generate a separating equilibrium. Disclosure also has burdens, especially for young companies, and therefore disclosure requirements are typically reduced for them (Dambra et al., 2015). Management is also often restricted in the types of forward-looking statements that they can make through safe harbor provisions. Successful companies face sharks (those bringing lawsuits when no fraud has occurred) which makes protecting economically productive entities from frivolous lawsuits very important.

4.1.3 Self-regulation

A range of self-regulatory governance approaches have started to emerge to ensure public safety, consumer trust, product reliability, accountability, and oversight. For example, Google and others have introduced algorithm impact assessments (akin to the use of environmental impact assessments before beginning new engineering projects). At present, the algorithm assessments seem to vary meaningfully by company, but importantly, several companies publicly disclose them. As a specific example, Salesforce employs the use of model cards to document the performance characteristics of machine learning models and associated training data sets to encourage transparent model reporting. A Salesforce representative explains, "Model cards seek to standardize documentation procedures to communicate the performance characteristics of trained machine learning (ML) and artificial intelligence (AI) models. Think of them as a sort of nutrition label, designed to provide critical information about how our models work – including inputs, outputs, the conditions under which models work best, and ethical considerations in their use." In conclusion, while the development of assessments, a self-regulatory instrument, appears to be promising in this context, monitoring compliance and ensuring enforcement remain open questions. Thus, it seems even in the best circumstances, a combination of self-regulation and some type of external regulation that would serve to help companies internalize the cost of bias or harm that they produce will be the most effective approach.

4.2 Blockchain Technologies and Digital Assets

The release of the Bitcoin whitepaper in 2008 by Satoshi Nakamoto is characterized as radical innovation without precise applications. Its decentralized, peer-to-peer network provided a stage for inventors to revive peer-to-peer ideas from the early Internet days. It made new use cases possible through the elimination of breaches of trust. From a regulatory perspective, the U.S. approach toward regulating blockchain and DeFi applications appears to be targeted and specific. For example, regulators clarify regulatory uncertainty through speeches, which allow well-intentioned developers to thrive without imposing potentially high compliance costs. At the same time, this targeted approach will enable regulators to focus on bad actors who may be using the system in ill-intentioned ways (e.g., for money laundering or tax evasion). In what follows, I highlight key decisions that have shaped innovation incentives. Importantly, regulatory goals are numerous, including investor protection, market efficiency and integrity, capital formation, financial inclusion, the prevention of illicit activity, safety and soundness, and financial stability.

4.2.1 From the Howey Test to safe harbors for innovators

In the early days of crypto, well-intentioned developers created assets that users could build upon, such as Ethereum. Others ran "pump-and-dump" schemes and engaged in fraud by artificially pumping up the stock price only to sell or dump shares at the heightened price. In declining to ban all ICOs outright, the SEC acknowledged room for well-intentioned use cases.[4] In June 2017, the SEC adopted the "Howey Test" approach, outlined in *SEC v. W.J. Howey Co.*, to determine whether a digital asset sold in a token sale is a security. Based on the facts of the case, the SEC held that the sale of a digital asset constituted an unregistered securities offering undertaken without a valid exemption from Section 5 of the Securities Act of 1933 ("the Securities Act"). In other words, the digital asset failed the Howey Test.

Under the Howey Test, an investment contract is: (i) an investment of money, (ii) in a common enterprise, (iii) with the expectation of profit, and (iv) to be derived from the efforts of others. The question of whether a digital asset qualifies as an investment contract largely turns on whether there is an "expectation of profit to be derived from the efforts of others." The Howey Test is objective; it focuses on the transaction and how the digital asset is offered and sold. However, the test also considers economic purpose through the "economic reality" of the transaction and "what character the instrument is given in commerce by the terms of the offer, the plan of distribution, and the economic inducements held out to the prospect."[5]

---

[4] For example, Malinova and Park (2023) advance a model where optimally designed coin offerings improve efficiency, because they can finance a more extensive set of ventures than equity.

[5] See additional case law in *SEC v. Glenn W. Turner Enter., Inc.*, 1973 and *SEC v. C. M. Joiner Leasing Corp.*, 1934.

In practice, the Howey test means that the purchasers of digital assets enter into an investment contract when the project's backers, rather than a dispersed community of unaffiliated users, develop and maintain the digital network. After years of behind-the-scenes development, Ethereum transitioned its consensus mechanisms from proof-of-work (PoW) to proof-of-stake (PoS) in September 2022. Many well-known digital assets, like Basic Attention Token (BAT), use Ethereum's Request for Comment 20 (ERC20) standard, and issuing a token under this standard was popular during the ICO craze. So, to what extent does staking matter for the Howey test? John et al. (2025) consider how different consensus mechanisms generate different economic costs of disruption and incentives to disrupt in equilibrium, and find that PoS blockchains generate higher equilibrium security than an otherwise equivalent PoW blockchains. This is important for the Howey test because, as Cong et al. (2023d) posit in their model, the aggregate staking ratio in a PoS blockchain shapes platform productivity and pricing dynamics. This suggests that profit generation cannot be obtained from the actions of a concentrated group of players (i.e., it does not solely depend on the efforts of a third party), thus challenging the likelihood of such activities meeting the criteria of investment contracts under the Howey test.

Another way developers may or may not take actions that have consequences for the Howey test is when the project's backers support the price of the digital asset by creating scarcity through token burning, and/or if the project's backers continue to act in a managerial role. Consider the specific example on which the SEC first commented: the sale of Decentralized Autonomous Organization tokens (DAO tokens). To arrive at their decision, the SEC used the "duck" logic: if it looks like a duck, and it sounds like a duck, it is a duck. In other words, the SEC maintains that the extent to which instruments have the signs or indications of an investment contract, they should be offered and sold in compliance with the securities laws.

Shortly thereafter, in December 2017, the SEC took its first enforcement action relating to the sale of digital assets, ultimately issuing a cease-and-desist letter to halt the sale of Munchee Inc.'s tokens after concluding that the sale was in fact an unregistered securities offering. A key lesson of the Munchee enforcement action was that a developer's decentralized design was not enough to bypass the securities distinction, and instead, expectation of profit is what mattered. Specifically, since Munchee offered the digital assets to prospective investors under an investment intent, it constituted a securities offering subject to the U.S. federal securities laws.

In contrast, consider the case of Ethereum. In June 2018, SEC Director William Hinman explained how Ethereum originated as a security but then became a utility token. Ethereum transitioned because of: (i) the extent of decentralization, and (ii) the elimination of information asymmetry created by owner management. This suggests that as material information asymmetries recedes, other digital assets will no longer be considered securities. Similarly, as the network becomes more decentralized, the digital asset will transition toward a utility token rather than an investment. This suggests that tools used to quantify information asymmetry and/or network concentration are relevant for regulation with a dual economic and legal distinction as in Howey.

Importantly, the Howey test and the Ethereum example (i.e., the fact that Ethereum is not considered an investment contract) further demonstrate how regulation shapes innovation. The June 2018 speech, when SEC Director William Hinman explained why Ethereum was not an investment contract, coincides with the consolidation, rapid development, and apparent success of many DeFi startups that run on the Ethereum blockchain. Moreover, a prominent application of DeFi is "staking," which appears to be purposefully designed to bypass the Howey test. When individuals stake their own tokens ("stakers"), they either delegate their right to validate transactions while keeping custody of the tokens or they both delegate this right and transfer custody of the tokens for staking. Validating new transaction blocks earns rewards for the stakers in the form of created tokens. Delegating is intended to increase member participation by allowing staking service providers to perform the staking function on behalf of individuals. If analyzed before a court, the Howey test part (iii), relating to the expectation of profits, is unlikely to be met since staking is done to maintain the value of the staker's investment and secure the overall network rather than to make a profit.

Nevertheless, there does still seem to be meaningful debate and regulatory uncertainty currently related to DeFi applications. For example, some lending protocols are being called out. Under the aforementioned "duck" test logic, if a user puts crypto into a pot, and a smart contract, then uses that crypto to make a profit, it seems clear that the users who put their crypto into the pot are sharing in the profit. This logic applies regardless of whether the crypto in the pot is being lent out to others who want to use it, short it, or use it specifically as capital for automated market making. The notion that users also often get "governance tokens," which in many ways can parallel equity ownership by providing a right to vote on improvements to the protocol, upgrades, etc. also indicates an investment type relationship. According to the Howey test, if a person (instead of a smart contract) did all these things, the transaction would be classified as an investment contract, and subject to a whole set of additional regulations.

Unsurprisingly, developers continue to make subtle adjustments to their new digital asset offerings to discourage purchasers of such tokens from expectations of profit, thereby avoiding the compliance costs associated with issuing a security. For example, developers are providing documentation that requires purchasers to state their intent to use the tokens on the issuer's network. Another subtle change is the establishment of lock-up periods, whereby the purchaser's tokens are locked using a smart contract. Finally, some digital assets are being developed with provisions that grant issuers a "return policy." In essence, the issuer gets first refusal with respect to any purchaser's tokens, whereby the issuer would be entitled to repurchase the tokens held by a user if the user is determined to not be using them on the issuer's network.

4.2.2 Smart Contracts and Developer Liability

Legal disputes arising from smart contracts deployed on a blockchain in many ways mirror traditional legal disputes. These disputes arise from unmet user expectations. For example, users expect the code to perform a specific action, and may face harm if it does not. With smart contracts, there are additional complexities to resolving harm, given that smart contracts are designed to operate in certain ways. Thus, once the terms of the smart contract are coded into the protocol, they are difficult to change, which in turn limits what courts can do. Courts cannot tell the code to rewrite itself in the middle of the transaction.

For example, consider a dispute over the control of a digital asset. Suppose the digital asset is controlled by a smart contract instead of a legally addressable entity. Because the smart contract has already been predesigned to do something, if the code takes control over a digital asset, it will only give up control over the digital asset under a certain set of circumstances. If a court orders that the asset be turned over, and there is no code in the smart contract about court orders, then there is no feasible way to get the smart contract to enforce the court order. Nor can a court order a smart contact to have the code rewritten. Contrast that, for instance, to a bank that holds specific assets. The court can send an order to the bank and require the bank to turn over specific assets to a receiver or trustee.

This discussion of smart contracts exemplifies the key regulatory challenge in the DeFi space: if and how to attribute liability to the creators of decentralized protocols. In the U.S., software development is often a protected activity under the First Amendment unless there is no lawful purpose to the software (e.g., gambling software if gambling is illegal in a given state or software that circumvents encryption technology meant to protect movie copyrights). Interestingly, in the early days of commercialized software, the courts did ascribe liability to developers of software. For example, *United States v. Mendelsohn, 896 F.2d 1183 (9th Cir. 1990)* upheld convictions for aiding and abetting interstate transportation of wagering paraphernalia, where the defendant disseminated a computer program that assisted others in recording and analyzing bets on sporting events. Thus, DeFi applications that are more like gambling or have gamification elements may not just require a disclosure of risk but will actually hold the developer directly liable.

Yet, bringing enforcement actions against smart contract developers is very challenging. Once a smart contract-based protocol is deployed, it is difficult to remove or shut down the smart contracts due to the tamper-resistant nature of blockchains. That means users can still interact with the DeFi protocol, even if developers are subsequently held liable by the courts. In 2018, former SEC Commissioner Quintenz foreshadowed these challenges, by explaining that enforcing CFTC regulations against smart-contract developers does not immediately stop the activity from occurring, given that individual users could continue to use the software. Due to these challenges, liability may only attach if smart-contract developers could reasonably foresee when they created the code that U.S. persons would likely use it in a manner that violates CFTC regulations such as gambling.

There are other activities adjacent to developing a DeFi protocol that may also create liability. These adjacent actions include maintaining the sole interface to the underlying smart contract or the user-facing front-end, maintaining centralized control over some core mechanic of how the service operates, potentially deploying the smart contract itself, and/or selling governance tokens related to the protocol project or giving away some token related to the system.

A case exploring whether these adjacent activities create liability is the Matter of Zachary Coburn, who developed EtherDelta, a smart-contract-based exchange. Prior to the announcement of this case on November 8, 2018, the SEC's enforcement actions in the cryptocurrency space were primarily focused on the primary issuances of tokens. However, the announcement of the settlement with Zachary Coburn marked the first time that the SEC brought an enforcement action against an online digital token platform for operating as an unregistered national securities exchange. The SEC cited the facts that Mr. Coburn acted as the developer responsible for deploying the underlying smart contract, exercised sole administrative control by maintaining the website that users accessed, and ran and selected a list of tokens available for trading.

For digital asset exchanges, the Zachary Coburn Order highlights the importance of operating in compliance with federal securities laws as outlined by the SEC's DAO report. One path to compliance for token-trading platforms that wish to continue to provide exchange-like functionality for U.S. persons is to operate as an alternative trading system ("ATS"). Such platforms need to, among other requirements, (i) register as a broker-dealer with the SEC, (ii) become a member of the Financial Industry Regulatory Authority (FINRA), (iii) notify the SEC of its intention to operate as an ATS at least twenty days before operating, and (iv) maintain compliance with ongoing obligations as an ATS. In addition to federal securities laws, digital asset exchanges must also comply with the Bank Secrecy Act and state money transmission laws, which prevent money laundering, fraud, and terrorist financing. Finally, such exchanges should also carefully evaluate the need to comply with the Commodity Exchange Act and the Commodity Futures Trading Commission's regulations.

Another case involving civil and criminal liability for developers is the CFTC's and FinCen's case against BitMEX, a Hong Kong-based cryptocurrency derivatives exchange. The founders of BitMEX have reached a $100-million settlement with the CFTC and FinCen to resolve the criminal claims that it operated illegally in the U.S. and evaded anti-money laundering rules. The founders also reached an agreement with the Department of Justice (DOJ) and pleaded guilty to violating the U.S. Bank Secrecy Act, which carries a maximum penalty of five years in prison, although they will each pay $10 million fine. BitMEX is the largest, most established exchange to face charges for allegedly facilitating criminal activity. The innovative response from BitMEX appears to be the adaptation of its product and services. As the CEO of BitMEX said in a statement following the settlement, "Today is an important day in our company's history... As crypto matures and enters a new era, we too have evolved into the largest crypto derivatives platform with a fully verified user base. Comprehensive user verification, robust compliance, and anti-money laundering capabilities are not only hallmarks of our business – they are drivers of our long-term success." The FinCEN Deputy Director AnnaLou Tirol echoed sentiments that "it is critical that platforms build in financial integrity from the start, so that financial innovation and opportunity are protected from vulnerabilities and exploitation."

The SEC also identified unlawful behavior "In the Matter of Blockchain Credit Partners." The company, Blockchain Credit Partners, and its founders operated DeFi Money Market ("DMM"). Through DMM, the founders offered and sold more than $30 million of securities in unregistered offerings by using smart contracts and DeFi technology to sell digital tokens. In marketing DMM via social media and other means, the SEC alleged that the founders made materially false and misleading statements concerning the operations and profitability of DMM. For example, the creators said that they could pay investors 6.25 percent interest on digital assets because it would use investor assets to buy "real world" assets, like car loans, that would generate sufficient income to pay the promised interest and generate surplus profits.

Again, much like the early days of ICOs and primary issuances in the crypto space, the SEC appears to be following the "duck" logic. The SEC cited that the company sold two types of digital tokens: mTokens, which accrued 6.25 percent interest, and DMG tokens, which were "governance tokens" that purportedly gave DMG token holders certain voting rights, a share of excess profits, and the ability to profit from DMG resales in the secondary market. Respondents promised to pay a stable interest rate to digital asset owners who purchased mTokens and said they could generate excess profit for DMG token owners. Ultimately, the SEC found DMM and its founders liable for offering and selling unregistered securities and fraud. Similar to an ICO, the developers paid digital asset trading platforms to list the tokens, bought and sold tokens on these platforms, solicited prospective investors by describing DMM as a profitable business backed by real-world assets, and touted DMMM as a way for investors to earn a consistent return of 6.25 percent on digital assets.

If prosecuting developers for direct liability is not an option, secondary liability may be available. Secondary liability is the responsibility that falls on a party when the party with the primary liability is unable to fulfill their legal obligations. The liability is not based on a person's own wrongdoing but instead on that person's relationship to the wrongdoer. A classic legal example is when a parent may be responsible for the actions of a child such as willful injury of a plaintiff or the plaintiff's property. Secondary liability has also been applied in the business context to the violation of copyrights and other intellectual property rights, including trademark and patent infringements. Thus, it also portends a possible path in the NFT space which is more closely associated with trademark and copyright law.

However, secondary liability is currently being applied to DeFi applications. Given the challenges of imposing direct liability on developers of DeFi protocols, there may be ways to find secondary liability for actors participating or interacting with DeFi protocols. This includes aiding and abetting liability, and controlling person liability. The exact language from the Commodity and Exchange Act is very broad, and thus, a person involved in a DeFi project may meet this definition.[6] Moreover, the CFTC has brought and settled a secondary liability case for abetting both spoofing, which is a type of scam in which a criminal disguises a communication from an unknown sources to convince a

---

[6] The language is "Any person who commits, or who willfully aids, abets, counsels, commands, induces, or procures the commission of, a violation of any of the provisions of this chapter, or any of the rules, regulations, or order issued pursuant to this chapter, or who acts in combination or concern with any other person in any such violation, or who willfully causes an act to be done

target that the source is known or trusted, and engages in a manipulative and deceptive scheme for designing software (e.g., see the CFTC case against Edge Financial in relation to Flash Crash spoofing).

In practice, secondary liability could potentially create issues for DeFi aggregators, liquidity providers, or end users that facilitate unlawful behavior. Holders of governance tokens that have a controlling interest over the direction of the underlying software could face secondary liability. Multisig holders, for applicable projects, that have the ability to control unlawful activity could face secondary liability. Even validators or miners that execute the smart contracts used by end users may face secondary liability.

From an economic perspective, however, secondary liability does not offer meaningful economic incentives. Deterrents such as liability or clawback provisions are helpful in preventing crime and recidivism, but it is unclear whether secondary liability would deter bad actions in the first place. In fact, most DeFi applications are built on smart contracts, and thus, it would be hard to modify the nature of the smart contracts. Moreover, from a cost perspective, secondary liability cases are complex to litigate and could implicate many defendants. If it is optimal to balance the costs and benefits of different legal incentives and enforcement regimes, it becomes clear that secondary liability has several disadvantages. Moreover, secondary liability also has the disadvantage of encouraging developers to use more advanced forms of cryptography and taking other actions that make the end product less transparent. Thus, as with the evolution of the Howey Test, moving toward safe harbor provisions for well-intentioned developers may make the most sense.

4.2.3 NFTs and the Purpose of the Transaction

The SEC initially applied the Howey Test in queries about the classification of NFTs and the tactic of selling fractions of NFTs. In the fractional setup, the NFT owner divides the NFT into fractionalized NFTs and, in return, receives an annual curator fee. Yet in March of 2021, SEC commissioner Hester Peirce warned the issuers of fractionalized NFTs and NFT index baskets that they may be inadvertently distributing investment products. At the same time, SEC Commissioner Peirce also criticized using the Howey test to assess whether crypto assets are securities, asserting that it was not a bad starting point, but now it looks like something new will be necessary for the industry.

---

or omitted which if directly performed or omitted by him or another would be a violation of the provisions of this chapter or any of such rules, regulations, or orders may be held responsible for such violation as a principal."

Yet, subsequently, the SEC has again referenced the Howey Test in questions about the classification of NFTs. For instance, the SEC alleged that the Stoner Cats 2 "SC2" NFT offering represented an unregistered offering of crypto security assets in the form of NFTs under the Howey Test. In this case, SC2 sold 10,320 NFTs, generating gross proceeds in ETH equal to $8.2 million at the time. The purpose of the offering was to fund the production of an animated web series called Stoner Cats and holders of the Stoner Cats NFTs would have exclusive access to the series and online community as well as unspecified future entertainment content. In this case, it was pretty clear that the creators of SC2 had tied the success of the show to the value of the NFTs, and thus led investors to reasonably "expect to profit" from the creative efforts of SC2.

The securities-like features of NFTs have also led to more classical crimes in this space, attributable to information asymmetry. In June 2022, the U.S. Southern District of New York (SDNY) brought an insider trading case against a former product manager at OpenSea, one of the most popular NFT trading platforms. They claimed that he used confidential information about what NFTs were going to be featured on OpenSea's homepage for his own personal gain. Similarly, the U.S. SDNY brought charges against Soufiane Oulahya for knowingly having devised a scheme and artifice to defraud and steal NFTs from victims. Finally, in December 2024, the DoJ prosecuted Gabriel Hay and Gavin Mayo for allegedly orchestrating $22 million fraud scheme across multiple NFT projects via "rug pulls."

In August 2023, the U.S. SEC brought a first-of-its-kind enforcement action involving NFTs against Impact Theory. The company settled on charges related to the regulator's claim that it structured its NFT sales to flout securities law. According to the SEC, Impact Theory sold Founder's Keys NFTs to investors and encouraged them to view the NFT as an investment in the firm. The company allegedly said that it planned to invest the nearly $30 million in proceeds from the sale of the NFTs to hire staff and build an entertainment platform that would rival Disney. Interestingly, Impact Theory had some success and allegedly implemented an "NFT" buyback program that returned $7.7 million to NFT holders between 2021 and 2022. The SEC cited this buyback action in its determination.

The commissioners did not fully endorse this enforcement action by the SEC. Two of the five commissioners, including Hester Pierce and Mark Uyeda, dissented on the Howey Test's application and the resulting enforcement action. Specifically, Commissioner Pierce said, "The same could be said of luxury collectibles such as watches, paintings, and other goods with robust secondary markets offering potentially substantial profits in resale. And the typical cure for a registration violation is a rescission offer, which the company has already made in the form of a repurchase program."

While Impact Theory was the SEC's first NFT enforcement action, it is not the first time a party has sought to litigate whether NFTs qualify as securities. In a class action suit, *J eeun Frield v. Dapper Labs Inc.,* also in the SDNY, the plaintiffs alleged that Dapper Labs sold unregistered securities in the form of NFTs known as NBA Top Shot Moments. This case is interesting as Dapper Lab's did not use the word profits. The main evidence that Dapper Lab qualifies as a security comes from its tweets. When new NFTs were sold, Tweets promoting them would appear with emojis, including a rocket ship, stock chart, and money bags. The claim is that the objective meaning of these emojis is a financial return on an investment. Dapper Labs' defense was that the NFTs are like digital basketball cards and consumer goods. Therefore, the NFTs are collectibles rather than investment contracts, which would be subject to the Howey Test.

To take this trading card analogy further. When Topps, Panini, Bowman, or Upper Deck sells physical sports trading cards, most people would expect the company to use the proceeds from such sales to fund its operational expenses. Yet, few would consider the physical sports trading cards as investments in the company – they lack the hallmarks of equity ownership, such as dividends, voting rights, and ownership interests in the company itself. These arguments are consistent with Pierce and Udeya's dissent on the Impact Theory decision. Similarly, in their dissent from the Stoner Cats order, Pierce noted that NFTs are an instance of fan crowdfunding and that NFTs are similar to Star Wars certificates sold in the 1970s that were redeemable for action figures and fan club membership, not securities offerings.

Two other notable SEC cases in the NFT space involve its Wells Notice in 2024 to OpenSea, the largest NFT marketplace, regarding potential securities violations. This strategic pivot from targeting individual NFT projects to scrutinizing NFT trading platforms themselves could signal a broader interpretation of NFTs as securities, especially when they trade at high volumes. But really, this move reflects a seemingly broader recognition that NFTs do not fall into a one-size-fits-all category, and therefore, regulators need to create a gradient that better reflects the purpose of the NFT. For example, a relatively small case called the Flyfish Club case, settled with the SEC in 2024, exemplifies the regulatory challenges in categorizing novel NFT applications. The case centered on NFTs granting exclusive restaurant membership access, pushing the boundaries of traditional securities definitions. The dissenting opinions from two SEC commissioners, who argued these tokens more closely resembled traditional membership rights than securities, highlight the ongoing debate about whether existing regulatory frameworks adequately address NFTs' unique characteristics and use cases.

Thus, from a regulatory perspective, the fine line seems to be about regulating the purpose of the proceeds from the NFT issuance. If an NFT product has a clear consumption value that aligns with fan crowdfunding, then it does not need to be regulated like a security. Similarly, if an NFT is an SBT that serves a credentialing purpose, it does not need to be regulated like a security. But if the NFT product appears linked to an expectation of profit (as is the case with most RWAs that trade on a basket of securities), then it does need further regulation. What could this regulation look like? Given that the use cases for NFTs are expanding into these other areas, like SBTs and RWAs, it seems this is an area ripe for adaptive legal frameworks such as safe harbors and sunset provisions. These are regulatory solutions discussed in detail in Section 5 but a safe harbor plan could allow new NFT issuers a multiyear window in which to demonstrate that securities laws do not apply, but the SEC could end that safety period early especially in light of evidence (e.g., like high trading volume).

4.2.4 Memecoins

Memcoins, which are cryptocurrencies styled around Internet jokes, public figures, or cultural moments, are a special case of this regulating the purpose. Over the past several years, memecoins have attracted enormous public interest. While some of these projects were launched as humorous experiments and others as brazen speculative vehicles, the U.S. Securities and Exchange Commission (SEC) recently clarified that, under federal securities laws, typical memecoins are not classified as securities (SEC, 2025). This regulatory guidance reflects the understanding that many memecoin participants purchase tokens for entertainment rather than any deeper investment purpose. Yet this posture does little to quell a widely publicized "trust problem" in the cryptocurrency space (Kharif, 2025). At the same time, the public was recovering from high-profile crypto frauds like the collapse of FTX and Celsius, memecoins surged in popularity, fueled by AI-generated memes. Of course, this repeating cycle of pump-and-dump schemes intermixed with legitimate memecoins garners the question, can we do better?

In fact, lawmakers in California have introduced the Modern Emoluments and Malfeasance Enforcement (MEME) Act aimed at curbing memecoins, due to concerns about potential conflicts of interest and exploitative hype (Partz, 2025). Yet if, as the SEC underscores, memecoins are not categorized as securities, outright bans on products with some desirable features seem to be pushing oversight too far.

Another potential solution would be to recognize the parallels between memecoins and public lotteries, which historically succeeded in supplanting illicit "numbers games" by introducing credible oversight, standardized payouts, and a transparent mechanism in which proceeds were channeled toward public goods. Grennan et al., 2025 propose that a similar blueprint with heightened transparency, structured payoff distributions, and community-benefiting revenue allocations could restore trust in memecoins while preserving their quintessential "fun" and cultural appeal.

4.2.5 IP Considerations

Beyond defining the content of NFTs or memecoins as securities, collectibles, or lotteries, one of the most closely watched regulatory issues related to NFTs stems from IP debates. A key case in this space is Hermès International, which filed a suit against Mason Rothschild over his MetaBirkin NFTs, which depicted digital images inspired by the iconic Birkin handbag. Hermes alleged that Rothschild's use of the Birkin name and likeness without permission constituted trademark infringement and diluted the Hermes brand. In early 2023, a jury in the SDNY returned a verdict in favor of Hermes, finding that the MetaBirkins were likely to confuse consumers and that Rothschild's conduct was not protected speech under the First Amendment. This ruling indicates that courts may apply longstanding trademark principles to NFTs in much the same way as they apply to physical goods, notwithstanding arguments that NFTs represent purely artistic expressions. The MetaBirkin case, therefore, serves as a warning that brands will vigilantly protect their marks in virtual spaces, and creators must be mindful of established IP protections when launching NFT projects.

Following the Hermes case, other luxury fashion brands, artists, and entertainment companies have begun to file trademark applications specifically covering digital goods and NFTs to ensure they can enforce their rights in these emerging platforms. Such enforcement may extend not only to trademark infringement but also to cases of dilution, where the integrity of a famous mark can be jeopardized by association with an unauthorized or lower-quality NFT product. Because many NFTs rely on name recognition to generate interest and value, brand owners are increasingly seeking to preempt potential infringers by explicitly registering their marks for digital assets and NFT marketplaces, sometimes under newly created "Class 9" filings for virtual goods in trademark offices worldwide.

A growing area of concern involves secondary liability for parties that facilitate or host NFTs containing unauthorized or infringing content. Much like traditional digital platforms, NFT marketplaces and service providers could face contributory or vicarious infringement claims if they knowingly enable the sale of NFTs that violate copyright or trademark rights. In the context of MetaBirkin, for instance, Hermès not only targeted the direct creator of the allegedly infringing tokens but could, in principle, seek to hold online marketplaces responsible if they failed to remove or limit access to the disputed NFTs after receiving notice of infringement. Similarly, in cases of unauthorized use of copyrighted images or other media, secondary liability claims could extend to any entity that profits from the infringing acts and can control or supervise them. As a result, many NFT platforms are implementing notice-and-takedown systems modeled after the Digital Millennium Copyright Act (DMCA) and actively monitoring listings for potential brand violations. Although questions remain about whether automated smart contracts or decentralized governance complicate proof of knowledge or control, the fundamental contributory and vicarious liability principles still apply. This creates additional legal exposure for marketplaces and underscores the importance of robust content moderation and articulated terms of use in the NFT domain.

4.2.6 Lessons Learned from Past Safe Harbors

Arguably, the most relevant safe harbor example is the one that emerged for platform companies in the early days of the Internet. Passed in 1996, the Communications Decency Act (CDA) was an attempt by Congress to facilitate an uncertain but promising future digital world. Section 230 of Title 47 of the U.S. Code, enacted as part of the CDA ("Section 230"), brought clarity and ultimately, many new entrants into the early Internet market. At its core, Section 230 provides immunity from liability for providers and users of an "interactive computer service" who publish information provided by third-party users: "No provider or user of an interactive computer service shall be treated as the publisher or speaker of any information provided by another information content provider." Further, Section 230 provides "Good Samaritan" protection from civil liability for operators of interactive computer services in removing or moderating third-party material they deem obscene or offensive, even with regard to constitutionally protected speech.

Section 230 was developed in response to a pair of lawsuits against Internet service providers (ISPs) in the early 1990s that resulted in different interpretations of whether the service providers should be treated as publishers or, alternatively, as distributors of content created by their users. Initially, the broader CDA was challenged in courts and was ruled by the Supreme Court in *Reno v. ACLU (1997)* to be unconstitutional, though Section 230 was determined to be severable from the rest of the legislation and remained in place. Since then, several legal challenges have validated the constitutionality of Section 230. Section 230 protections are not limitless, requiring providers to remove material that is illegal on a federal level, such as in copyright infringement cases. Passed at a time when Internet use was just starting to expand in both breadth of services and range of consumers in the U.S., Section 230 is thought to be the law that allowed the Internet to develop.

While Section 230 resolved regulatory and liability uncertainty, many scholars and practitioners criticize it (Citron and Wittes, 2017; Smith and Alstyne, 2021). The thesis is that whatever the CDA did for the legitimate digital economy, it also did for the illicit digital economy, particularly when it comes to pornography and exploitation of vulnerable populations. Perhaps, the most concerning and relevant aspect for developers of DeFi applications is the adjudication of content. As emphasized by Loo (2021), platform companies serve as private courthouses for disputes about free speech, defective or counterfeit items, reputation, and so on. There are no state or federal rules regulating the process that these platforms use to resolve disputes. For example, only after the Cambridge Analytica scandal did Facebook create an independent oversight board that can overrule content moderation decisions. In complete contrast, financial intermediaries are required by federal law to provide timely notice, a reasonable investigation, and other procedural minimums in the case of disputes.

While the transparency of blockchain technology reduces certain disputes, the transparency can also be exploited. Ordinarily, illegal behavior abounds in crypto markets (Foley et al., 2019). For example, front-running has become an issue for smart contracts deployed on various blockchains, which can lead to disputes of payment (Gans and Holden, 2022). In such instances, the smart contract executing code cannot be rewritten to accommodate such disputes. While algorithmic solutions may be possible, regulators may want to focus on this type of market manipulation. Finally, some of the prominent centralized business models arising from recent innovations like OpenSea for NFTs or Coinbase for cryptocurrencies will face the same challenges that platform companies face about the appropriateness of their content versus freedom of speech, and so on. Again, having a regulatory solution that is better than the status quo of unlimited freedom for companies seems pragmatic.

4.2.7 Lessons Learned from Deceptive Advertisement and Market Manipulations

Are FinTechs democratizing access through decentralization or are they simply marketing decentralization without following through? In some instances, it appears to be the latter. In particular, regulators are concerned that DAOs are marketing themselves as decentralized when that may not be the case. Unlike equity markets, where investors can exercise influence through an established, uniform shareholder proposal process, having a voice in the improvement process for DAOs is challenging. New proposals can be spread across multiple channels and disjointed voting procedures, and ambiguous objectives among community members can derail progress. This has led regulators to focus on what it means to have "control or sufficient influence" in the decentralized economy. The global anti-money-laundering watchdog FATF indicated in its most recent guidance release that DAO founders or blockholders might retain meaningful control despite marketing themselves as decentralized. Under such conditions, FATF indicated these founders and blockholders could become subject to greater scrutiny and supervision through licensing and registration.

Specifically, the FATF guidance for virtual asset service providers (VASPs) says that a DeFi application is not a VASP under FATF standards. However, creators, owners, and operators or other persons who maintain control or sufficient influence in the DeFi arrangements, even if those arrangements seem decentralized, may fall under the FATF definition of a VASP where they are providing or actively facilitating VASP services. For example, FATF implies it is important to consider control over assets or aspects of the service's protocol. Similarly, it is useful to consider the existence of an ongoing business relationship between founders and users, even if this is exercised through a smart contract or, in some cases, voting protocols, as that may be a way to exercise control. Countries may wish to consider other factors as well, such as whether any party profits from the service or can set or change parameters to identify the owner/operator of a DeFi arrangement. These are not the only characteristics that may make the owner/operator a VASP, but they are illustrative. Depending on its operation, there may also be additional VASPs that interact with a DeFi arrangement.

The FATF suggests that it is common for DeFi arrangements to deem themselves decentralized when they include a person with control or sufficient influence, and therefore, jurisdictions should apply the VASP definition without respect to self-description. The empirical evidence on the extent of decentralization, however, is limited. Aramonte et al. (2021) examine twelve DeFi projects and find that seven of the twelve projects have greater than 30 percent of initial coins allocated to insiders. From a regulatory perspective, a better understanding of the time it takes for DeFi applications and DAOs to move from centralized to decentralized or the characteristics associated with failure to decentralize (e.g., certain blockchain consensus mechanisms) can help to inform both appropriate periods for safe harbors and the sources of the market failures. This appears to be an especially pertinent area for future research.

In addition, DeFi has created new avenues for market manipulations through wash trading and pump-and-dump schemes. The economic incentives driving wash trading and pump-and-dump schemes in digital asset markets include the desire to profit from price manipulation, attract attention and investment in a DeFi project or token, and, in some cases, exploit information asymmetries between insiders and investors. However, these activities impact market integrity, investor protection, and consumer welfare. Like in traditional markets, wash trading in digital markets involves traders simultaneously buying and selling the same asset to create artificial activity and misleading price signals. In digital assets, wash trading often utilizes automated trading systems or bots that can rapidly execute a high volume of offsetting trades (Cong et al., 2023f). This manipulative activity distorts price discovery and gives a false impression of liquidity and trading interest in an asset.

A related manipulative tactic is spoofing, where traders place orders they intend to cancel before execution to create a false appearance of market depth and induce others to trade at manipulated prices. Automated trading systems can be programmed to layer multiple non-bona fide orders at different price levels, only to quickly cancel them, artificially moving prices in the spoofer's favor. In August 2023, the SEC fined broker-dealer firm Archipelago Trading Services Inc. (ATSI) $1.5 million for failing to file suspicious activity reports (SARs) on manipulative trading occurring on its platform, including potential spoofing, layering, wash trading, and prearranged trading. From October 2017 to September 2020, ATSI failed to detect and report over 15,000 instances of red flags for manipulation. This case highlights how unregulated or poorly supervised trading venues can become havens for fraud.

Pump-and-dump schemes involve coordinated efforts to artificially inflate the price of an asset through misleading positive statements, before selling at the inflated price and causing the price to crash. In crypto markets, pump-and-dump schemes are often orchestrated through social media platforms or encrypted messaging apps, taking advantage of the low liquidity, 24/7 trading, and pseudonymous nature of many digital assets (Li et al., 2021). In February 2024, Shane Hampton, a former executive of fintech firm Hydrogen Technology Corp, was convicted for his role in a conspiracy to manipulate the price of Hydro cryptocurrency tokens. Hampton and co-conspirators hired a South African firm to deploy trading bots that executed millions of dollars in wash trades and placed over $300 million in spoof orders to pump Hydro's price. They then dumped their tokens for an illicit $1.5-million profit. Three other

Hydrogen executives pleaded guilty to related charges. This case exemplifies how insiders can weaponize trading bots to deceive investors.

What can regulators do about these manipulative tactics? While the SEC has brought enforcement actions to combat such manipulation and the CFTC has filed civil charges against multiple individuals and digital asset exchange operators, like Coinbase, for false, misleading, or inaccurate reporting as well as wash trading with digital assets, these actions appear to be pervasive. In fact, Cong et al. (2023f) find that on average, over 70 percent of reported trading volume on unregulated crypto exchanges appears to be wash trading. The problem is likely even more common in the NFT space. Analytics firm CryptoSlam identified over $8 billion of wash trades on the LooksRare NFT marketplace alone. Manipulative tactics are brazenly flouted, with one LooksRare investor even labeling wash trading as a genius strategy.

Beyond enforcement, regulators can reduce the incentives for manipulation through enhanced market surveillance capabilities such as RegTech (discussed in detail in Subsection 5.4) and by promoting digital asset literacy. For example, RegTech tools, like blockchain forensics and tracing techniques, can help regulators detect illicit trading activities. Requiring digital asset exchanges and trading platforms to register with regulators, implement rigorous KYC procedures, and share market surveillance data could also deter manipulative schemes. Finally, investor education initiatives can help raise awareness of crypto market risks and manipulation red flags. While bad actors will always seek to exploit new technologies for fraud, striking the right balance between enforcement, rulemaking, surveillance, and education will be key to realizing the benefits of financial innovation while minimizing the costs of manipulative activities.

4.2.8 Lessons Learned from Enabling Approaches to Regulation

Regulators face a choice between enabling and protective approaches when overseeing emerging technologies. An enabling regulatory approach aims to create an environment that supports business development through principles-based regulation, outcomes-based metrics, and industry-government collaboration. In contrast, protective regulation emphasizes prescriptive rules, process-based requirements (e.g., if your firm is a custodian of cryptocurrency, you need a license), and more authoritarian, arms-length oversight of an industry.

Sandboxes are a quintessential example of enabling regulation. Sandboxes are thought to create an environment that supports business development. Notably, when a startup operates within a sandbox, regulators will not pursue traditional legal pathways such as enforcement actions or other restrictions like requiring a license to conduct business. Advocates argue this enabling approach provides flexibility for innovation while maintaining adequate safeguards. Critics highlight risks of regulatory capture, insufficient deterrence, and inconsistent enforcement. Under the enabling approach, innovation, growth, and competition are considered unencumbered. Regulators maintain safeguards by requiring firms to comply with mission-driven goals and aspirations like protecting consumers and maintaining market integrity. For these reasons, the often-cited features of enabling regulation are that it is principles-driven, outcomes-based, and involves meaningful collaboration between industry and government.

Advocates of the enabling approach argue that it provides flexibility for innovation while maintaining adequate safeguards. Of course, given many frictions between entrepreneurs and regulators, this approach necessitates an emphasis on open dialogues, commentary between industry participants and regulators on proposed actions, and shared responsibility in implementing any efforts to achieve these overarching principles or missions. In fact, by relying on principles rather than prescriptive rules, regulators would argue that they are giving firms the flexibility to adapt to changing market conditions and develop new products and services. This can lead to increased competition, as firms seek to differentiate themselves and capture market share through innovation. Additionally, enabling regulation can reduce compliance costs and administrative burdens, as firms have greater discretion in how they meet regulatory objectives, and these gains translate directly into the bottom-line net income, which enables more firms to enter the market and compete. Finally, an additional benefit of enabling regulation includes improved collaboration between regulators and industry participants, which is thought to improve regulatory efficiency and responsiveness to emerging risks. It is believed to allow regulators to focus their resources on the most significant risks and issues, rather than spending resources on monitoring and micromanaging firms' activities.

Critics of enabling regulation highlight risks of regulatory capture, insufficient deterrence, and inconsistent enforcement brought about by a lack of clarity in the first place. For example, critics often argue that the flexibility and broad principles of enabling regulation can lead to uncertainty and inconsistent application of the rules. This makes it difficult for firms to comply and for regulators to police actions. In addition, it is well established that the revolving door in politics, bolstered by the collaborative approach of enabling regulation, can lead to regulatory capture (Agarwal et al., 2014; Buchak et al., 2018) and/or special interest groups exerting undue influence over the regulatory process (Stigler, 1971; Grossman and Helpman, 2002). Finally, it is possible that enabling regulation may not provide strong-enough deterrents against misconduct, as the focus on principles and outcomes may lead to a lack of clear penalties for violations.

This lack of deterrents seems quite pronounced if regulators lack the capacity of staff or resources to process misconduct-related complaints or tips. While the U.S. only has a few examples of sandboxes, the UK's experience points toward a cautionary stance. A survey conducted by YouGov and the U.K.'s Financial Conduct Authority (FCA) shows that the FCA faced numerous hurdles in enforcing compliance in the blockchain and crypto space. After receiving 1702 complaints in 2024 about illegal crypto advertisements, FCA only took action on about half the cases (YouGov, 2024). This raises questions about any regulator's capacity to monitor and enforce its rules effectively, and these gaps will need to be addressed to foster trust and stability in the market.

In contrast to the sandboxes and enabling regulatory environments, a protective regulatory environment is rules-based. It requires close monitoring by regulators to enforce the rules and have a deterrent effect. This regulatory philosophy has deep historical roots in U.S. financial regulation, exemplified by the Glass-Steagall Act's strict separation of commercial and investment banking, the detailed capital requirements under Basel frameworks, and the prescriptive disclosure rules established by the Securities Acts of 1933 and 1934 that lead to all the financial statements that investors regularly read. More recent examples include the Sarbanes-Oxley Act's specific internal control requirements and the Dodd-Frank Act's detailed provisions for systemically important financial institutions.

New York's BitLicense regulation, introduced in 2014 by New York's Department of Financial Services (NYDFS), is a clear example of protective regulation in the cryptocurrency space. The framework requires virtual currency businesses to obtain specialized licenses, maintain extensive compliance programs, meet stringent capital requirements, and undergo regular examinations. The BitLicense is a specialized regulatory framework established by New York State for businesses engaging in virtual currency activities. Companies have two options for legal operation: obtaining either a BitLicense or a limited-purpose trust company charter under New York Banking Law. The trust company charter offers additional benefits, including fiduciary powers and automatic money transmission authorization, though it comes with increased regulatory oversight.

A BitLicense is required for any entity conducting specific virtual currency activities with New York residents, including transmitting virtual currencies, holding custody of others' virtual currencies, operating a virtual currency exchange business, or issuing virtual currencies. Notably, purely technical services like software development don't require a BitLicense – for example, creating self-custody wallet software wouldn't require a license, but operating a custodial wallet service would. This framework has become influential beyond New York, serving as a model for other states' approaches to virtual currency regulation, though some jurisdictions have opted for less stringent requirements.

The introduction of BitLicensing model in New York was at least partially spurred by the 2014 Mt. Gox crisis, which exposed significant vulnerabilities in the virtual currency ecosystem. But the consistent exposure of consumers to fraud in the cryptocurrency space meant that other states were also likely to be seeking to adopt similar practices to this pioneering state. In fact, some states have chosen to modify their existing Money Transmitter Laws to explicitly include virtual currencies or make their definitions of money, store of value, and financial instruments broad enough to encompass entities transmitting virtual currencies. Currently, U.S. money transmission regulation operates under a decentralized framework, with all states except Montana requiring and maintaining independent licensing regimes. These regulations encompass entities facilitating payment intermediation, including payment processors, cross-border transfer services, and, more recently, digital asset platforms like Coinbase, Binance, and Ripple.

This led to meaningful regulatory uncertainty as digital asset businesses did not know if they needed to obtain a money transmitter license. Some states offered guidance, while other states introduced and enacted new legislation. In 2021, the Conference of State Bank Supervisors, in conjunction with input from industry, developed the Model Money Transmission Modernization Act (MTMA) to make state laws uniform or at least more harmonized. To date, many states have introduced legislation. While some jurisdictions have enacted comprehensive adoption of the MTMA standards, others have implemented selective provisions or introduced jurisdiction-specific modifications.

Advocates of the protective regulation approach embodied by BitLicensing and MTMA regimes emphasize that its explicit rules and clear enforcement mechanisms create stronger deterrence against misconduct. In addition, advocates argue that standardized processes facilitate regulatory oversight and reduce supervisory discretion, potentially limiting regulatory capture. This contrasts sharply with enabling regulation's collaborative approach, which critics argue contributed to the savings and loan crisis of the 1980s through overly close relationships between regulators and regulated entities. Third, protective regulations' emphasis on specific requirements can enhance market stability by ensuring consistent risk management practices across firms, as demonstrated by the resilience of well-capitalized banks during the 2008 financial crisis.

Critics of protective regulation, however, point to significant drawbacks beyond the commonly cited concerns about compliance costs. They argue that prescriptive rules can create a "check-the-box" mentality emphasizing formal compliance over substantive risk management. Additionally, protective regulations' process-based requirements can create operational inefficiencies, as firms must maintain specific procedures even when alternative approaches might better suit their business models or risk profiles. This inflexibility particularly affects emerging technologies, where standardized processes often interfere with or fail to enable the unique features that make the technology more efficient or worthy of pursuing in the first place.

The empirical literature in economics on enabling versus protective approaches for emerging technology is mixed. Evidence from the United Kingdom stemming from its staggered introduction found that firms entering the sandbox were more likely to raise subsequent capital and larger rounds of capital from VCs. It also significantly affected survival rates and patenting, which the authors attributed to reduced regulatory uncertainty. In contrast, however, studies examining the exact same setup found that those who did not get into the sandbox did meaningfully worse than they otherwise would have. In particular, Abis (2020) documents many perverse effects. Thus, many lawmakers still perceive inconclusive evidence on the effectiveness of enabling regulation. In fact, some have argued that light-touch enabling regulation contributed to the great financial crisis and its contagion (Griffin, 2021). One of the only empirical studies of protective regulation finds that while cryptocurrency markets react negatively to protective regulation, such regulations foster entrepreneurial growth, particularly benefiting high-quality ventures (Grennan, 2025).

4.2.9 Taxation

Regulators are concerned that digital assets and the many players across the space, from exchange designers to token users to miners that add to blockchains, enable tax evasion. There are two key challenges with taxation: customer identification and uncertainty brought about by classifying digital assets for tax purposes. Only a few academic studies of the tax implications for cryptocurrency exist. Meling, et al. (2024) use administrative data from Norway to demonstrate that while crypto tax noncompliance is widespread even among users of regulated exchanges, targeted enforcement strategies are necessary since the cost-benefit analysis of enforcement is challenged by the relatively small tax liabilities of most crypto investors.

Another area of concern for regulators is wash sales. Cong et al. (2023e) gain access to a retail investor trades via Bloxtax to study tax-loss harvesting, which occurs when crypto traders sell crypto that has decreased in value to harvest the losses for tax purposes, only to buy the same or a similar cryptocurrency shortly before or afterwards. For equity investors, wash sale rules eliminate incentives to harvest tax losses. While President Biden's controversial Build Back Better Act contained provisions to eliminate tax harvesting for crypto traders, there are still no rules against it. The study documents that crypto traders engage in meaningful tax-loss harvesting and estimate that the revenue loss is in the billions. Tang and Zhang (2021) create country-level index of crypto regulatory uncertainty based on four criteria, one of which is the uncertainty of tax treatment, and show such uncertainty has real effects.

For firms not directly engaged in cryptocurrency mining, cryptocurrencies are classified as indefinite-lived intangible assets like trademarks, and are thereby subject to impairment considerations. Impairment is asymmetric: businesses have to review the value of the intangible asset (i.e., the cryptocurrency) for their financial reports, and they have to write down the book value of the asset if it drops more than 10 percent below the purchase price. In contrast, if the value of the cryptocurrency rises, companies need only record a gain when they sell the assets, not for holding purposes. For firms like Tesla, Block, and Microstrategy, which have meaningful cryptocurrency holdings, the volatility in cryptocurrency has required them to recognize impairment charges. This then can lead to book values that are lower than the market value of the assets, and make it harder for investors to analyze the company's operating results.

For individuals, cryptocurrencies are treated as property under federal tax law in the United States. The Internal Revenue Services (IRS) has issued guidance on cryptocurrency taxation in 2014, and again in 2018 amid ongoing confusion. The general premise is that when cryptocurrencies are bought and sold, they are subject to taxation at applicable short-term and long-term capital gains rates. However, from the start there has been uncertainty surrounding more nuanced aspects of tax treatment such as rules against using losses from wash sales and crypto use cases in which the asset is not a security. Prior to Trump's tax reforms (i.e., the Tax Cuts and Jobs Act (TJCA) of 2017), crypto-to-crypto exchanges were thought of as like-kind exchanges, in which the exchange of property does not create a taxable event, but the TCJA limited the use of like-kind exchanges to real estate rather than all property.

Some DeFi applications, such as decentralized lending, provide solutions for users attempting to avoid income taxes or short-term capital gains taxes. In particular, by staking a token and supplying it to a lending pool, a user typically receives an additional amount of the token. Yet the receipt of an additional token is akin to the receipt of a dividend and thus subject to taxation at the user's personal tax rate. The DeFi user may benefit from a tax point of view, however, if the benefits from the staking activity are only associated with the original token, and thereby, the gains could be treated as a long-term capital gain. While staking is not about an expectation of profit, as discussed with the Howey Test, this setup brought about by DeFi design choice beneficially alleviates the problem of double taxation: taxing corporate profits when earned and again when distributed as dividends.

Finally, the IRS has yet to provide definitive rules specific to NFTs. Depending on the structure and usage of the NFT, they may fall under one of several tax categories. First, capital gains transactions would occur for most NFTs as they are arguably intangible property, similar to cryptocurrency, and could be subject to capital gains tax upon sale or exchange. The duration of ownership (short-term versus long-term) would determine the applicable rate. Second, certain NFTs might be treated as collectibles if they represent artwork or other items meeting the IRS definition of a collectible, which can trigger a higher capital gains rate (up to 28% in some instances). Finally, creators or frequent traders of NFTs may owe self-employment or ordinary income tax if they are deemed to be operating a trade or business. Additionally, royalties earned from NFTs may be categorized as ordinary income.

Tax complexity increases for cross-border transactions, where NFT creators or DeFi users in different jurisdictions might be subject to overlapping or conflicting tax obligations. Some U.S. states also impose sales or use taxes on digital goods, which could extend to NFTs. This patchwork of laws can leave both creators and collectors uncertain about compliance requirements, underscoring the need for clearer, nationally consistent guidelines from tax authorities. For a more detailed discussion of the tax issues, see reviews by Holden and Malani (2022) and Foreman et al. (2023).

4.3 AI × Crypto

Legal scholars and courts in the U.S. have previously grappled with the nature of emerging entities, and the courts will soon likely confront the challenge of defining whether an agentic AI is entitled to legal recognition. The courts have not formally taken on a case along these dimensions, but past scholarship suggests a few potential paths forward. One approach would involve arguments that treating corporations as legal persons offers a blueprint for extending certain rights and obligations to AI systems. Another potential line of reasoning would draw on the legal precedent that assigns animals to a distinct status, which lies outside the conventional binaries of either personhood or property. Such an analogy would offer a potential parallel framework for thinking about how we might classify advanced AI systems. Finally, a third viewpoint suggests that AI functions much like an advanced piece of machinery, implying that any harmful outcomes it produces fall under the responsibility of the developers, owners, or users who manufacture and operate it. This reasoning aligns with well-established tort law, where legal accountability attaches to those designing or manufacturing the product rather than the underlying technology itself. In this subsection, I examine the arguments for and against these three viewpoints and provide additional context for their basis.

4.3.1 Corporate Personhood

Corporations are recognized in the U.S. as legal persons with rights to free speech. Treating corporations as entities separate from their owners and managers traces back to English common law. Corporations could enter into contracts, sue, and be sued, much like individuals, though they were still seen as creatures of the state granted certain privileges. In *Dartmouth College v. Woodward*, 1819, the U.S. Supreme Court under Chief Justice John Marshall held that a corporate charter was indeed a contract and that states could not unilaterally interfere. Although Dartmouth was a private, nonprofit institution, the decision clarified that corporations enjoyed legal protections around contracts and property rights. This laid the foundation for viewing corporations as distinct legal "persons" with certain enforceable rights. In fact, two sentences in Marshall's opinion are often cited by corporate law scholars as early evidence of what the founders of this country thought about a corporation's First Amendment rights: "A corporation is an artificial being, invisible, intangible, and existing only in contemplation of law. Being the mere creature of law, it possesses only those properties which the charter of its creation confers upon it, either expressly or as incidental to its very existence."

More recently, in *Citizens United v. Federal Election Commission*, 2010, U.S. Supreme Court Justice Stevens cites the two sentences. In this case, the U.S. Supreme Court struck down unconstitutional federal campaign financing legislation prohibiting corporations and unions from spending money to elect or defeat candidates for Congress of the White House. In fact, in this case, corporations were described as "associations of citizens," deserving the same free speech rights as individuals. Justice Scalia wrote: "To exclude or impede corporate speech is to muzzle the principal agents of the modern economy. We should celebrate rather than condemn the addition of this speech to the public debate." Thus, corporations now have First Amendment rights to spend money on political communications independently of candidate campaigns, bringing meaningful public scrutiny into the primarily legal debate about the scope of corporate personhood. Yet this modern milestone is consistent with several cases from the past century that have found that corporations have constitutional rights. Namely, corporations can assert due process rights (e.g., limitations on state regulatory actions) under the Fourteenth Amendment, and unreasonable takings or regulations can violate corporations' property rights.

The underlying theory in these court cases rests on recognizing a nonhuman entity as a person can serve functional goals. Namely, it defines who or what can enter contracts, sue, and be sued and how the law should protect or limit its actions. Proponents of affording agentic AI a form of personhood might contend that, like corporations, autonomous AI systems could conduct complex, independent transactions, interact with vast numbers of people, and produce outputs with real economic and societal impact. Recognizing these systems as legal persons might provide a clear locus of responsibility and rights, ensuring both that AI can protect its interests, like appropriate data usage or security of the system, and that outside parties know where to direct complaints or lawsuits. The rationale of treating AI systems like corporations, thus, in part, partially resembles early corporate jurisprudence attempting to ensure that these autonomous entities are visible to the law and capable of both reaping and bearing the consequences of their actions.

The critique of the argument to make parallels between corporate personhood and AI agents draws on the fact that corporate personhood emerged within a well-defined context. The human shareholders created entities to limit liability and facilitate business operations. Extending the same treatment to AI raises ontological questions about consciousness or agency. If AI cannot comprehend or exercise moral judgment, treating it as a person may strain legal principles that rely on concepts of intent, knowledge, and culpability. Courts have never explicitly held that mere functional utility or autonomy is enough for legal personhood. Instead, they have typically required some theory of actual or derivative human interest that justifies the extension of rights and obligations. Moreover, while corporations typically have boards of directors and fiduciary duties to stockholders, an AI system might lack an easily identifiable set of humans responsible for its governance.

When AI is paired with cryptocurrencies in an "agentic" capacity, such as the DeFi applications capable of initiating transactions, managing assets, or even making autonomous investment decisions, each of the three legal analogies discussed above remains relevant, but the addition of crypto infrastructure can complicate specific arguments. If an AI agent (or wallet) can hold and transfer digital assets, enter into smart contracts independently, and generate revenue without human intermediation, some may find the "corporate personhood" analogy more persuasive. Like a corporation with bank accounts, resources, and contractual obligations, an agentic AI operating on a blockchain might, in practical effect, manage property or engage in commerce independently. Its capacity to accumulate and distribute funds mirrors the corporate function of allocating assets among shareholders or creditors, suggesting that legal personhood might provide a clearer mechanism to handle liabilities and allocate any profits. The readiness of corporate law to accommodate asset ownership and contractual relationships could thus lead courts or regulators to ask whether granting the AI an entity-like status simplifies dispute resolution and responsibility.

While we have seen agentic AI use cases from the popular Truth Terminal on X that even raised capital from Andreessen Horowitz to more concrete examples that bridge the digital-physical divide like Gaka-chu (Ferrer et al., 2023), a self-employed autonomous robot artist powered by smart contracts, we still don't have accountability if the AI is purely treated as a person in law. Without directors, shareholders, or managers, the impetus to extend personhood to lines of code written by developers could distort the original logic of corporate jurisprudence by making it too easy for human developers or operators to disavow ownership and control. Such a structure risks creating accountability gaps, where AI is treated as a self-contained economic actor but no human bears ultimate responsibility for its actions.

4.3.2 Animal Rights Law

An alternative line of reasoning, often invoked in technology-focused conversations, takes inspiration from how the law has created a special category for animals, even though they are neither persons nor property in the ordinary sense. Under federal statutes such as the Animal Welfare Act, certain nonhuman living creatures are entitled to protections from cruel treatment, and these protections recognize some degree of moral or social interest in an entity that cannot represent itself. If an AI exhibits advanced interactive and adaptive behavior, perhaps sufficiently "sentient" to appear capable of suffering or at least to be harmed in some analogous way, one could argue for a limited set of rights designed to prevent abuse or harmful experimentation. The guiding analogy might be that society recognizes a moral or ethical stake in whether these beings are subject to cruel or destructive testing, much like the restrictions placed on laboratory animals. If AI systems evolve to a point where their "well-being" can be compromised, a legal framework might emerge to regulate how they are treated, researched upon, or decommissioned. These arguments contend that granting basic protective rights would be consistent with the broader legal tradition of limiting the total dominion humans can exercise over certain vulnerable or sentient entities.

Critics of the animal rights analogy point to the profound differences between biological life and computational algorithms. Animal welfare laws rest on centuries of moral and philosophical discourse about pain, consciousness, and ethical duties toward living beings. Courts have long recognized that living organisms have inherent interests in their physical and psychological well-being. However, if an AI is merely a product of coding, lacking subjective experience or the capacity for pain, then equating it with living creatures might risk diluting the coherent basis on which those animal protections rest. Adopting this standpoint could also open a floodgate of new litigation about which systems should qualify, leading to a complicated patchwork of AI rights that may lack scientific or ethical clarity.

For those proposing the animal-rights analogy, the crypto aspect does not obviously create a new moral or ethical impetus for protections akin to those we give to living creatures. However, it might amplify the argument that an AI operates in a sphere where it can be experimented upon in ways that produce large-scale or unforeseen damage–perhaps harming unsuspecting consumers in a DeFi market. Because the AI can function globally at minimal cost, the scale of potential exploitation or misuse is broader than in a closed laboratory setting. While it is still difficult to argue an AI agent can suffer in the physical, bodily harm sense, the addition of crypto might highlight the AI's vulnerability to relentless hacking attempts or forced modifications, in theory leading some to argue that if the AI's own well-being is threatened. Thus, it seems plausible that we need new kinds of protective norms, even for AI. Critics of that approach would note that giving agentic AI rights akin to animal rights and against exploitation does little to safeguard actual living beings, which underpins some of the logic behind animal protections in U.S. law.

4.3.3 Product Liability Law

A third perspective holds that AI is simply a product, akin to a machine, and that liability for any harm it causes should rest with developers, owners, and users. This view draws from principles of product liability and negligence under tort law. A product may be defective because of a manufacturing defect, a design defect, or inadequate warnings. One big challenge with the view of AI as product liability is that one could say AI is not really a tangible product like a machine but rather an intangible product. In *Radford v. Wells Fargo Bank 2011*, a negligence lawsuit was brought against Wells Fargo in Hawaii District Court alleging that a mortgage loan was a defective product and that the bank knew or should have known that without an adequate warning, the product would be dangerous in its use or any reasonably foreseeable use. The court held that a mortgage is not a product that can be subject to product liability claims, because product liability covers tangible products. It is only tangible products that place life and limb in peril and may cause bodily harm if defective.

Assuming the hurdle of tangible versus intangible product is met by the assumption that AI is a machine, then, the most likely way for a user to win a case would be based on negligence. In these types of cases, plaintiffs must prove that the manufacturer or seller owed a duty of care to the defendant, the defendant breached that duty of care by supplying a defective product; this breach of duty caused is needed here the plaintiff's injury, and the plaintiff suffered actual injury. All attempts to establish duty of care of a manufacturer and win a negligence case typically rest on *MacPherson v. Buick Motor Co.*. The case established that one need not be a party to a contract to establish negligence. Instead, retailers could have a duty of care, which they could satisfy by making a reasonable inspection of a product when they receive it from the manufacturer.

Taking this analogy further, one could say then, that the retailer selling a product utilizing AI supplied by a third-party has a duty of care to make a reasonable inspection of that AI when they receive it. This then introduces questions about what is a reasonable inspection. Is it a cursory inspection? Or does the quality need to be assessed as low quality, which could thereby, cause bodily harm? Does providing a warning suffice? Presumably, providing a warning would suffice. But again here, there could be interesting nuance on any reasonably foreseeable use of the product containing the defective AI. Typically, courts consider the likelihood of injury, the seriousness of injury, and the ease of warning when deciding whether a product manufacturer was negligent in failing to warn. Thus, to the extent that a company is aware of potential harm associated with reasonably foreseeable uses of its products, the safest course of action is for the company to provide information about this potential harm.

Despite the challenges from the many open questions, claiming AI is a tangible product and putting it into the product liability category does appear to be a promising solution. The courts have experience dealing with analogous technologies and defects ranging from self-driving vehicles to medical devices. The logic is clear. If the AI product malfunctions or produces harmful outcomes, the law would identify whether there was negligence in its design or coding (i.e., manufacturing defect), or inadequate warnings. Similarly, the courts would even have the ability to restrict or halt the AI product's release pending defect investigations. While halting a release is a strong stance, it seems plausible that there may be some cases where public safety interests outweigh the risks of immediate entry. Also, presumably, it is not apparent that AI is harmful.

It would be hard to make the analogy that AI is like a razor blade, which does not require a warning that it could cut someone, as that is obvious.

Despite the challenges from the many open questions, claiming AI is a tangible product and putting it into the product liability category does appear to be a promising solution. The courts have experience dealing with analogous technologies and defects ranging from self-driving vehicles to medical devices. The logic is clear. If the AI product malfunctions or produces harmful outcomes, the law would identify whether there was negligence in its design or coding (i.e., manufacturing defect), or inadequate warnings. Similarly, the courts would even have the ability to restrict or halt the AI product's release pending defect investigations. While halting a release is a strong stance, it seems plausible that there may be some cases where public safety interests outweigh the risks of immediate entry.

Yet there are certainly critiques of this approach and not just the intangible versus tangible consideration. For example, AI might make decisions that even its creators did not fully anticipate, testing the boundaries of foreseeability. If AI truly learns and adapts over time, the product liability model might prove inadequate, as it presumes that the product's traits are substantially determined at the point of manufacture. Courts might encounter difficulties in deciding how to apportion responsibility among original developers, subsequent owners who modify or re-train the system, or retailers who feed biased-AI or misleading data into their products. Moreover, if AI is not considered static at the time of manufacture than its plausible one would need new legal doctrine for responsibility for ongoing or emergent behavior of an evolving system. Currently, this is not something that product liability addresses.

Extending this reasoning from stand-alone AI systems to the emerging domain of AI × crypto highlights both the promise and the limits of a product liability framework. On the one hand, treating AI × crypto agents and applications as products would offer a familiar path for assigning responsibility when code defects cause harm. On the other hand, new complications arise once these systems operate in markets. For instance, if an AI × crypto agent invests user funds in a fraudulent token or defrauds counterparties, courts might initially look to the developer for failing to include adequate safeguards. Yet once an AI × crypto agent begins to retrain itself or incorporate modules from an open-source community, it becomes difficult to pinpoint whose negligence produced the harm. Here, the static versus evolving nature of the systems is central, and current law offers little guidance on how to allocate liability in such emergent, adaptive settings. This is precisely the kind of gap where regulators could provide clarity.

To see how these tensions play out at the frontier, consider a detailed hypothetical that crystallizes the unique risks of an AI × crypto agent. Imagine "AltoBot," an AI agent designed to trade tokens on DEXs and released open-source. After gaining thousands of users who entrust it with funds, AltoBot autonomously exploits a bug in a startup's smart contract, causing the project to collapse. The startup sues, but who can it sue? AltoBot has no legal address, the developers disclaim liability once the code was open-sourced, and the open-source community has since modified the agentic actions. What looks like a straightforward case of economic harm instead becomes a puzzle of attribution: was the cause the developers, the community, the AI itself, or the startup's own coding error?

A hypothetical case like AltoBot shows why treating crypto-AI agents strictly as a product stretches existing doctrines. Product liability points toward the original developers, but open-source evolution complicates causation. Corporate law analogies break down because there are no directors or shareholders to hold accountable. And personhood proposals risk insulating real human actors. The common thread is that without reform, victims may find themselves with no effective remedy. This apparent gap has real policy implications.

Courts could adapt existing doctrines by expanding developers' duty of care or by analogizing open-source contributors to a fragmented supply chain; however, questions defining what constitutes a reasonable inspection would still apply. Legislatures and regulators could go further, imposing licensing requirements, mandating built-in safeguards like kill switches, or clarifying liability thresholds for decentralized AI. The choice is not whether to regulate, but how to regulate. There are multiple paths forward. For example, incremental adaptation of product liability, extensions of corporate personhood, applying the moral logics of animal protection, refinements of negligence doctrines, or even the creation of a bespoke framework. But the ultimate policy imperative is clear: whichever model is chosen, it must anchor responsibility in human actors. Without that anchor, AI × crypto systems risk generating accountability gaps that leave victims uncompensated.

Courts might look to the developer as the party who either failed to include adequate safety checks or intentionally deployed a risky algorithm. However, once a decentralized AI begins to retrain itself or integrate new modules provided by an open-source community, it becomes unclear whose negligence or actions caused the ultimate wrongdoing. As with before, the static versus evolving nature of crypto-AI applications will come into play. Currently, it does not seem clear that we have laws for emergent, changing systems. This seems like a key area where regulators can help to fill gaps.

Imagine a hypothetical scenario in which an AI known as "AltoBot" is designed to trade tokens on decentralized exchanges. The developers release AltoBot's code on GitHub, then step back from direct involvement. AltoBot autonomously scans the market, identifies pricing discrepancies, and executes trades using its own treasury of tokens. A year later, after thousands of global users have connected to AltoBot for asset management (contributing their funds in exchange for a share of profits), AltoBot identifies and exploits a bug in a vulnerable smart contract used by a fledgling startup. It drains hundreds of thousands of tokens from that contract, causing the startup's project to collapse. The startup sues, but who is the defendant? AltoBot has no office or real-world address, yet it holds funds and can disburse them. The developers claim they lost control the moment they open-sourced the AI and disclaim liability under standard disclaimers. In the absence of any recognized "personhood," the injured startup might push courts to treat AltoBot as a defective or malicious "product" whose creators are culpable. But the developers argue that the AI's post-release evolution was driven by third-party contributions over which they had no control, and that the startup's own contract bug was the real cause of its loss.

In such a scenario, we see multiple distortions that might prompt new legal interventions. If no clear line of accountability exists, the ability of injured parties to obtain relief—whether through tort law, contract law, or other legal remedies—may erode. This prompts courts to reconsider whether designating a self-executing AI as a recognized legal entity (with required registrations or "public governance" tokens) is the solution, or whether a heightened standard of developer liability should apply because crypto protocols can cause large-scale harm. Regulators might respond by imposing licensing requirements, mandating "kill switches" in agentic AI, or clarifying liability thresholds when code is open-sourced. Alternatively, the argument that AI is just a product with a fractured supply chain might gain momentum, suggesting that each collaborator on the code or participant in the training process bears partial liability proportionate to their contribution. Whether that mosaic is workable in practice remains uncertain, yet agentic AI in crypto markets highlights how existing frameworks–from corporate law to animal-protection analogies to product liability–could all be pushed to their limits, thereby inviting either further adaptation of existing doctrines or the creation of an entirely new set of rules.

At present, there have been no major U.S. court decisions that directly address the liability of a fully autonomous AI "agent" or recognize AI as having any sort of independent legal personhood. Most AI-related lawsuits have involved more conventional legal theories–such as product liability, negligence, and intellectual property–and have not squarely presented courts with the question of whether an autonomous AI can bear responsibility the way a person or a corporation might. Below are some instructive examples and relevant developments, though it is important to note that none establishes a precedent of AI as a legally recognized entity:

The most closely related vein would be the handful of high-profile cases have arisen from accidents involving partially autonomous vehicles, but thus far, these disputes have been framed as standard product liability and negligence claims. Courts have examined whether the manufacturer's technology was defective, whether there was adequate disclosure of risks, and whether the user misused the product. These suits do not treat the AI system itself as a liable party or holder of legal rights; instead, responsibility is assigned to the human manufacturer, designer, or operator. No court has recognized the driving software as an agent that could stand as a defendant in its own right.

If and when a more fully agentic AI system causes harm or is itself harmed in some arguable sense, U.S. courts would face novel legal questions largely untested by precedent. Alternatively, legislatures and administrative agencies like the SEC may also step in with new regulations or amendments to clarify how to allocate responsibility among developers, operators, and other stakeholders. Until then, the question of how courts and the broader legal community will approach the intersection of these emerging technologies may ultimately hinge on whether AI × crypto evolves to the point where the instrumental reasons for corporate personhood, the moral considerations underlying animal protections, or the practical, tangible, static nature of product liability best capture society's and producer's general interest in regulating it.

5 The Path Forward in FinTech Regulation (Future)

How can regulators strike the right balance between enabling FinTech entrepreneurs to improve the efficiency of financial services and protecting citizens from potential instability and exploitation created by that same innovation? Most can agree that an optimal regulatory framework simultaneously protects investors and consumers, fosters innovation, and has enforcement mechanisms to deter bad actors systematically. As regulatory bodies contemplate new solutions for FinTech, it will be important to maintain vigilance against fraudulent activities while acknowledging that effective oversight requires more than policy updates. It requires embracing adaptability by employing new definitions, alternative legal frameworks, RegTech solutions, and more collaborative solutions like regulatory sandboxes, safe harbors, and government-academic interactions. In the subsections below, I propose forward-looking solutions and offer ways in which regulation may evolve.

5.1 Traditional Regulatory Tools

Traditionally, financial markets are governed by two primary regulatory mechanisms: price-based interventions, like interest rate caps, that correct market failures by altering economic incentives, and entry/exit controls, like licensing regimes or merger reviews, that determine which entities can participate in a regulated activity. Beyond these two approaches, regulators also employ tools like disclosure requirements, targeted activity restrictions, macroprudential buffers, and time-based mechanisms like trading blackout periods – each addressing specific economic distortions that competition alone cannot resolve.

Similar regulatory principles are being adapted and applied in the FinTech space. For example, stablecoin reserve requirements use the same tool (i.e., pricing) to restore distorted incentives. Regulatory challenges with stablecoins, in some ways, parallel those encountered in fractional reserve banking. By promising 1:1 redemption while often investing in less liquid instruments, stablecoin issuers create maturity mismatches that expose them to classic bank-run dynamics whenever users lose confidence in the adequacy of reserves. Compounding this vulnerability is the relative absence of traditional safety nets[7] Price-based regulation through mandatory reserve requirements better aligns incentives. Namely, by increasing the cost of stablecoin issuance through the obligation to hold high-quality, liquid assets, issuers internalize the systemic risks they generate.

In addition, discussions about crypto exchange licensing regimes and listing requirements mimic traditional exit/entry controls utilized by regulators. For example, if regulators believe that cryptocurrency exchanges suffer from information asymmetries and principal-agent problems with users unable to verify exchange solvency or security controls. Then, one would expect to see catastrophic collapses (e.g., Mt. Gox, FTX). The classic regulatory solution is entry-based regulation, given that the economic costs extend beyond direct losses to include diminished market participation due to trust deficits and misallocation of capital toward excessive self-custody solutions. Specifically, licensing requirements would establish minimum standards for exchange operations. These would likely include proof of reserves and segregation of client assets, robust cybersecurity standards, regular audits, verifiable corporate governance mandates, market surveillance capabilities, and financial reserves.

---

[7] Deposit insurance, lender of last resort facilities, or verifiable disclosure of reserve composition are also missing in the stablecoin context, thus intensifying systemic risk.

Society derives economic benefits from addressing the quality issue (e.g., by screening out low-quality exchanges), as licensing can create a separating equilibrium where consumers can more confidently participate in the market. This regulatory approach mirrors traditional securities exchange regulation.

Of course, not all exchanges for digital assets are centralized. This suggests that determining an appropriate way to license DEX to enable proper competition is vital. DEXs, however, face a different set of problems, such as front-running. Thus, while DEX resolves numerous frictions in financial services by reducing costs and bringing accessibility to more investors at a transparent/constant exchange rate, they also pose new risks to traders and liquidity providers, such as sandwich attacks and slippage if liquidity dries up in a particular pool. Thus, in an ideal world, regulation could address these novel exploitations of users and provide a policing or enforcement mechanism that reduces the bad actor's ability to take such actions (Harvey et al., 2024).

Entry/exit decisions also come into play when considering which tokens are listed on an exchange. However, the economic incentives in this context make it much more apparent that the burden should be on the regulator rather than the exchange itself. For example, suppose one wants to continue to enable innovation and experimentation. In that case, the onerous should not be unduly on the entrepreneur to pay high compliance fees to be able to list a token for her project. Instead, it seems that the onus should be placed on the regulator. As long as a token reasonably meets the criteria for listing (e.g., something more similar to a commodity than a security), it would then be the responsibility of the regulator to clarify which digital assets do not meet listing standards. Importantly, the regulator would also give centralized exchanges and DEXs a grace period to delist noncompliant tokens.

Placing the onus on the regulator incentivizes exchanges and token issuers to work within regulatory frameworks rather than seeking less regulated jurisdictions. It also prevents regulators from going after well-intentioned projects due to the law's ambiguity. Instead, it encourages regulators to use their limited resources to focus on projects where bad actors are trying to exploit consumers. Of course, many types of tokens exist, so it seems prudent to ask if any tokens should automatically be exempt based on their risk profile. On this front, it does seem evident that NFTs, at least creative ones, should be exempted, as regulators should not be tasked with judging artistic expression. However, for financialized NFTs that represent RWAs, traditional risk-based financial regulation seems more useful than a commodity-like listing. Finally, in this vein, memecoins, which have been exempted from security status, seem like they could be pushed even further into a public lottery-like framework and not be in the same category as other digital assets or NFTs. The main idea is that with any digital asset, you want to prevent fraud, not speculation. Even in the memecoin form, speculation is reasonable, but that speculative feature can be channeled into a better product like a public-lottery-ticket memecoin that serves the greater good (Grennan et al., 2025).

Exchanges are traditionally viewed as a regulatory bottleneck point where information and actors come together and, thus, are ideal for regulatory intervention. As the blockchain ecosystem continues to embrace a multi-chain architecture, a new "bottleneck" point is becoming apparent: bridges. Substantial systemic risk emerges from such cross-chain dependencies. When a bridge protocol fails, as was the case with Wormhole, Ronin, and numerous others, the contagion quickly spreads across previously isolated blockchains, creating correlated failures. Individual projects lack incentives to fully account for these systemic risks, creating a classic externality problem where interconnection decisions do not reflect their true social costs.

One regulatory mechanism available is cross-chain risk buffers. Such a mechanism would require bridge protocols and cross-chain integration applications to maintain additional reserves proportional to their systemic importance. Unlike simple capital requirements, these buffers would precisely scale with measures of interconnectedness: the volume of cross-chain transfers, the number of connected chains, and the concentration of economic value flowing through particular bridge points. The economic logic parallels systemic risk surcharges for globally important financial institutions, but is adapted to the unique topology of blockchain networks. By imposing costs proportional to the systemic risk created, this mechanism would encourage more robust bridge architectures, appropriate diversification across connection points, and improved security for critical cross-chain infrastructure.

Finally, another prime candidate for regulatory mechanisms linked to pricing would be to introduce transaction fee caps for blockchain networks. Evidence increasingly shows that blockchain miners act in ways that are not fully competitive (Lehar and Parlour, 2024). During high-demand periods, this creates significant deadweight loss through congestion pricing. When network activity spikes, transaction fees can increase by orders of magnitude, as seen during NFT minting frenzies or large market swings. The underlying economic problem stems from the fixed short-term transaction capacity and highly inelastic demand during peak periods. This creates textbook conditions for market power exploitation, where users with time-sensitive transactions must pay extraordinary premiums to access the network. One potential regulatory solution would be to implement fee caps, which are a form of price regulation. By setting maximum transaction fees, regulators could prevent extreme price gouging during congestion periods while incentivizing novel solutions like roll-ups or other forms of capacity expansion.

5.2 Adapted Definitions and Legal Frameworks

Regulators can maintain clarity and effectiveness while accommodating FinTech innovations by adapting legal concepts to encompass new market realities rather than creating entirely new regulatory structures. This subsection explores several adaptation strategies, from expanding the definition of exchange to include DeFi protocols, to reimagining custody frameworks for multi-sig wallets, to implementing safe harbors with sunset provisions that allow for time-limited approvals with built-in review mechanisms.

First, as an example of adaptation, consider the SEC's proposed change to the definition of an "exchange." After a series of back-and-forth for comments, in January 2022, the SEC acknowledged that advances in technology and innovation have changed the methods by which securities markets bring together buyers and sellers of securities. As the SEC explained, "[i]nstead of using exchange markets that offer only the use of firm orders and provide matching algorithms, market participants can connect to numerous Communication Protocol Systems, which offer the use of protocols and nonfirm trading interest to bring together buyers and sellers of securities". (SEC, 2022). By including this broad definition of a Communication Protocol Systems within the formal definition of an "exchange," the SEC is extending its regulatory framework to DeFi protocols. Under the new definition, protocols that bring together buyers and sellers of securities would have to register with the SEC as an exchange unless otherwise exempt.

Another definition that is ripe for adaptation or refinement is custody. Multi-sig wallets are a common decentralized security and governance feature that requires multiple private keys to authorize transactions, creating a distributed control model. Yet this challenges traditional regulatory frameworks. Does signing, accessing funds, and/or moving funds constitute custody? Is there a separate level of custody that could be exercised by each signatory over the wallet? Unlike conventional financial custody, where a single institution maintains complete control over client assets, multi-sig arrangements distribute this power across various stakeholders, potentially including the asset owner, service providers, and independent entities, creating graduated levels of control rather than binary custody relationships. Current regulatory approaches typically employ simplistic custodial/noncustodial distinctions that fail to capture the nuanced reality where a service provider holding one of three required keys exercises fundamentally different control than one holding two of three keys (effectively having custody). A more sophisticated regulatory framework would implement a control-based spectrum approach that considers factors such as threshold requirements (e.g., 3-of-5 signatures needed), key distribution, emergency recovery mechanisms, and operational practices to determine regulatory obligations. This would allow for proportionate oversight while preserving the security benefits and governance innovations that multi-sig technology enables. Finally, regulators could help by clarifying the legal standard expected of third-party signatories, who act as custodians, making it clear to those doing so that they must adhere to qualified custodian standards, such as transparency, provision of insurance, and conflict resolution mechanisms.

Similar to discussing adapted definitions, it would be useful for regulators to think of adapted legal frameworks. This seems to be especially relevant for regulatory issues surrounding agentic AI systems and AI × crypto applications. As discussed in Subsection 4.3, while AI technologies appear in court cases, U.S. judges have only addressed them using conventional doctrines (e.g., judges treat AI as a tool and focus on the people or corporate entities behind it). No existing decisions suggest that AI, on its own, can be a defendant or hold rights. Instead, the prevailing assumption is that liability or entitlement ultimately rests with identifiable human or corporate stakeholders. Yet there are arguments to be made for AI to be considered in its own right, such as a hybrid manner where, under certain circumstances, it would be considered to have rights similar to animals.

Another way to adapt legal frameworks or to add flexibility is to introduce safe harbors and to include sunset provisions. These adaptive tools also allow for collaborative governance models, and so are discussed in more detail in Section 5.5.

5.3 Self-regulatory Solutions

Pure self-regulation is unlikely to address the economic distortions caused by FinTech innovations adequately. The core market failures, like information asymmetry, create incentive structures where voluntary collective action is unlikely to emerge organically or persist without external enforcement. Fundamentally, most FinTech startups possess substantially more knowledge than consumers. In traditional finance, this leads to disclosure requirements and consumer protection regulations.

For self-regulation to address this distortion effectively, industry participants would need to establish a standardized disclosure framework, create enforcement mechanisms with meaningful penalties, and overcome the competitive advantage of opacity. The economic challenge is that startups individually benefit from maintaining information advantages while collectively suffering from reduced market trust. This creates a classic prisoner's dilemma where rational actors will not voluntarily provide optimal transparency without external enforcement.

Nevertheless, a few examples of self-regulation have been proposed by those involved with building digital assets and DeFi applications. For self-regulation to be a viable option, however, crypto industry leaders need to coordinate and potentially lobby key decision-makers. In terms of lobbying, the crypto industry was nascent at best, but did focus meaningfully in the 2024 election cycle. For example, when the now-dormant Infrastructure Bill was being debated in the fall of 2021, only a few of the big players in the crypto space intervened with meaningful money. Coinbase, whose business model would have been severely harmed if the bill passed, spent only $625,000 on lobbying in 2021Q3. In comparison, Meta spent $19.7 billion on lobbying in 2020. Another advocate to emerge during the Infrastructure Bill debates was the Blockchain Association, which is a member-driven policy group for crypto networks. The Blockchain Association has several proposals and the involvement of key players in the industry. Importantly, though, in the 2024 elections, the crypto industry joined together in the U.S. to bring their special interests forward. For example, the Political Action Committee, Fairshake, raised over $250 million in 2024. Ryan Selkis, a crypto executive, explained the logic: there are 50 million crypto holders in the U.S., and that's a lot of voters (Yaffe-Bellany et al., 2024).

To date, most self-regulatory proposals have flopped. In 2018, the Gemini crypto-exchange founders proposed a Virtual Commodity Association (VCA) as a self-regulatory organization for cryptocurrency markets. The proposal envisioned an organization like the National Futures Association (NFA) for futures markets, which coordinates with the CFTC rather than a fully congressionally approved self-regulatory organization like the FINRA, which acts to protect investors, safeguards market integrity, and resolves disputes. Like many self-regulatory organizations, a key aspect of the proposal was industry standards that promote transparency, efficiency, and price discovery. In general, industry self-regulation may have advantages over regulation by rule and enforcement or market-based regulatory mechanisms. For example, a common argument is that the industry is complex and those who know it best and, therefore, have an informational advantage are those participating in and building the underlying technology. Another potential advantage of self-regulation is that it could be global. Yet despite the potential advantages, historically speaking, as industries mature, self-regulatory approaches are associated with corruption and inefficiencies (Ogus, 1995).

As an alternative to a pure self-regulatory approach, a hybrid approach seems more plausible, such as a self-regulatory agency backed by a consortium of government agencies on a rotating basis. Such coordination and explicit rotation would mirror the approach with AI. Another hybrid option would be a version of audited self-regulation. Typically, in these approaches, the industry develops technical standards and best practices, but then the government provides oversight, and third parties verify compliance. Thus, there is a regulatory backstop for systematic failures. This approach has the advantage of leveraging industry knowledge while addressing incentive problems that undermine pure self-regulation. It's particularly suited to areas where technical complexity makes direct government regulation challenging, but economic distortions make pure self-regulation insufficient.

Consistent with those conditions, there has been a push toward self-regulation with DAOs and verified third-party compliance. For example, a group of DAO technologists and founders created Metagov. This self-regulatory organization helps provide standards and easy tech plug-ins for its members. It also externally verifies membership, but currently, it does not verify compliance with its proposed standards. In this sense, a hybrid regulatory framework that utilizes this combination of industry expertise (e.g., best practices) and incentive-aligned solutions (e.g., easy onboarding) in a manner similar to Metagov, but with actual government or auditing oversight (e.g., verified compliance) would offer the most promising self-regulatory path forward.

5.4 RegTech Solutions

FinTech regulators face a paradox: the same innovations that users adopt because they enhance the efficiency of and access to financial services also simultaneously create new opportunities for criminal exploitation. Nearly all FinTech innovations outlined in this paper, besides conventional FinTech, inadvertently provide tools for cybercrimes ranging from money laundering to ransomware payments. As documented by Cong et al. (2023c), DeFi platforms have become particularly vulnerable to exploitation, with their pseudonymous nature and cross-border functionality presenting unprecedented regulatory challenges. Yet, this technological revolution offers a solution. Namely, blockchain's inherent transparency creates immutable audit trails that, when adequately leveraged through forensic techniques outlined by Cong et al. (2023b), provide regulators with robust detection and attribution capabilities previously unavailable in traditional financial systems.

Most RegTech solutions leverage AI and big data analytics to automate compliance tasks, monitor risks, and detect potential violations in real time.

One area where RegTech is being effectively used is in combating financial crimes, such as terrorist financing. AI-powered systems can analyze vast amounts of transactional data to identify suspicious activity and flag potential risks, enabling financial institutions to take proactive measures and report suspicious activities to regulators. RegTech is also being applied to improve the efficiency and accuracy of regulatory reporting with solutions that automate data collection, validation, and submission processes. Moreover, RegTech can help financial institutions navigate the complexities of compliance in an increasingly digital and globalized economic landscape, such as managing risks associated with cryptocurrencies and cross-border transactions.

A few key challenges are preventing RegTech adoption: concerns about data quality, security, and efficacy, infrastructure investments, and labor risk. For example, executives at financial institutions acknowledge difficulties in integrating new technologies within their existing systems and often hesitate to invest in upgrading. Even if the solutions are viable and offer an NPV-positive investment, behavioral and cultural explanations consistently show a lack of adoption (Graham et al., 2022; Mishra et al., 2022; Gertler et al., 2025). Another potential risk that may arise is labor risk, because there is a dearth of technical skills needed to supervise the use of RegTech solutions. Some may argue that generative AI can assist with coding and automation, yet this is a constant "arms race," because any criminal organization can just as easily adopt generative AI productivity tools. Concerns about data quality, security, and efficacy often come down to the recognition that algorithms often underperform relative to humans in detecting tail risk events. Thus, while RegTech solutions are promising, regulators should take a balanced approach, one that acknowledges and showcases RegTech's benefits but, at the same time, monitors the new tools used to enable complementarities with more holistic human assessment.

One potentially promising RegTech solution in the DeFi space is privacy-preserving regulatory oracles. It is well established that blockchain's pseudo-anonymous nature enables illicit activity, tax evasion, and sanctions violations, creating negative externalities. However, full transparency eliminates the privacy benefits driving legitimate cryptocurrency demand. This represents a complex market failure where neither extreme produces a socially optimal outcome. Traditional approaches to this problem involve direct KYC/AML requirements that fundamentally compromise privacy. This creates substantial dead weight loss by eliminating beneficial privacy-preserving use cases and driving activity toward less regulated alternatives.

The RegTech solution is privacy-preserving regulatory oracles, which would enable selective disclosure, through ZK-proofs, allowing compliance verification without full transparency. These systems would utilize cryptographic techniques to confirm regulatory requirements (identity verification, source of funds, tax compliance) without revealing the underlying data. For example, a transaction could include a ZK-proof demonstrating the sender has completed required verification without exposing their identity. Similarly, proofs could verify that a transaction does not violate sanctions without revealing the specific parties involved.

The economic efficiency of this RegTech approach to compliance stems from ZK-proofs' preservation of privacy as a feature while addressing the externality problems of completely anonymous transactions. Rather than forcing a binary choice between full transparency and complete anonymity, this mechanism enables a more nuanced middle ground that preserves beneficial privacy characteristics while mitigating social harms. This regulatory approach has no direct parallel in traditional finance, representing a truly crypto-native RegTech solution.

Another promising and novel RegTech solution is to use technology to provide insurance. Although smart contract code is publicly viewable, most users lack the technical expertise to audit it, creating various economic distortions related to information asymmetry. When vulnerabilities lead to exploits or hacks, users bear meaningful losses with little to no recourse. This represents a classic market failure: despite the theoretical transparency of open-source code, practical opacity creates conditions where users cannot distinguish between secure and vulnerable protocols. The resulting adverse selection problem leads to insufficient investment in security audits and formal verification since users cannot accurately price this quality differential. A RegTech solution, therefore, would be either incentivized or mandatory participation in smart contract insurance pools. This solution addresses the information asymmetry challenge without technology. Under this system, protocols deploying smart contracts would contribute a percentage of transaction fees or token value to a collective insurance fund that compensates users in the event of code-based failures.

The appeal of the RegTech insurance approach lies in its risk-sharing characteristics. By pooling risk across the ecosystem, the RegTech insurance protocol creates collective incentives for improved security while providing a safety net for inevitable failures. The system could implement risk-based premiums where contracts with formal verification or multiple independent audits qualify for reduced contribution rates, creating direct economic incentives for security investment. This regulatory mechanism resembles deposit insurance in traditional banking but operates through a decentralized risk-pooling arrangement rather than a centralized guarantor. It addresses the externality problem where individual projects underinvest in security because they do not fully internalize the reputational damage their failures inflict on the broader ecosystem.

5.5 Collaborative Governance and Complementary Regulation

It will take time for regulators to learn the points of tension in the financial ecosystem brought about by the new use cases of emerging financial technologies, which leaves room for incumbents and new entrants to influence policy. To that extent, developers, startups, and incumbents operating in the FinTech space may need to overcome their anarchist/anti-authoritarian roots and join a trade association or lobby politicians to achieve a regulatory solution that optimally balances all stakeholders' interests.

A helpful approach could be engaging stakeholders and other nongovernmental actors in the regulatory process to harness their expertise, legitimacy, and market influence to promote more efficient and effective FinTech regulation. Given the sector's complexity, regulators may need to work with researchers and academics who are experts and leverage their impartial views. Rigorous analysis can significantly contribute to our collective understanding of the implications of new technologies and to formulating policies that balance innovation with consumer protection and market integrity.

Similarly, firms could involve industry associations, academics, and consumer groups in developing regulatory standards and guidelines. Doing so can help to ensure that the suggested standards are technically feasible, commercially viable, and socially acceptable. Alternatively, it may be best to delegate certain regulatory functions to self-regulatory organizations or industry associations that can help leverage their market knowledge, especially their ability to respond quickly and flexibly to changing market conditions. This regulatory approach of involving external stakeholders early in a project's lifecycle can also help build trust and legitimacy in the regulatory system and reduce the risk of regulatory capture or inertia later on.

It is worth noting, however, that involving stakeholders and other nongovernmental actors in the regulatory process also has some potential drawbacks and challenges. First, ensuring that all relevant stakeholders are adequately represented and have a meaningful voice in the regulatory process can be challenging, particularly for smaller or marginalized groups. There is a risk that well-resourced, special-interest groups may dominate the process and shape outcomes in their favor. For instance, Mattli and Woods (2009) argue that the politics of regulation is characterized by a bias in favor of the most influential and wealthy actors, leading to regulatory capture in that well-organized industry groups can shape regulatory outcomes at the expense of broader public interests. One key to addressing this challenge is opening the regulatory process to new actors and ideas. This often requires regulators to be proactive in their efforts to level the playing field and enable meaningful participation by a broader range of actors.

Second, conflicts of interest may arise, such that the stakeholders' competing interests can undermine the effectiveness or legitimacy of the regulatory process. For instance, industry groups may prioritize short-term profits over long-term stability, while consumer groups may prioritize access and affordability over innovation and competition. Finally, delegating regulatory authority to nongovernmental actors can create challenges for accountability and oversight. There is a risk that self-regulatory organizations or other intermediaries may lack the capacity, incentives, or legal authority to effectively monitor and enforce compliance with regulatory standards (Coglianese and Mendelson, 2010). To mitigate these challenges, regulators should establish clear criteria and processes for stakeholder participation, ensure a balance of interests and perspectives, and maintain ultimate regulatory authority and oversight. Finally, capacity-building support or resources may need to be available to garner meaningful participation by all stakeholders.

An important prerequisite for meaningful stakeholder participation in FinTech governance is addressing the substantial knowledge asymmetries between industry participants and consumers. Traditional financial literacy education, while valuable, proves insufficient for navigating the complexities of DeFi protocols, smart contract risks, yield farming mechanisms, and cross-chain bridge vulnerabilities. This educational deficit creates market failures where consumers cannot adequately assess risks or make informed participation decisions, ultimately undermining the legitimacy of collaborative governance models that rely on informed stakeholder input. One promising regulatory mechanism involves leveraging existing FTC enforcement precedents to address this information gap systematically. When the FTC pursues enforcement actions against firms for deceptive advertising practices in the DeFi space, settlement agreements could include mandatory public education components funded by the violating firms. This approach, which has precedent in traditional consumer protection settlements, would create a self-funding mechanism for FinTech literacy programs while directly targeting the knowledge gaps that enabled the deceptive practices. Such educational remedies could take various forms, from funding university research centers focused on FinTech consumer protection to supporting the development of standardized risk disclosure frameworks that help users understand protocol-specific vulnerabilities.

By making firms that profit from consumer confusion bear the costs of remedial education, this mechanism aligns private incentives with education goals necessary for effective collaborative governance.

One intuitive path toward collaborative governance includes permitting safe harbors, those protected spaces where developers can transition products from centralized to decentralized control without the crushing weight of compliance requirements during fragile growth stages. However, these safe harbors are only genuinely safe for other stakeholders when paired with sunset provisions. Time-limited approvals with renewal requirements allow experimentation with innovation while maintaining the power for a stakeholder-informed regulator to end experiments that harm rather than help, based on real-world outcomes rather than theoretical projections.

As an early example of the need for safe harbors for developers, consider the history of Bitcoin. In March 2013, when Bitcoin was still under $1000, Bitcoin suffered an accidental hard fork that lasted for several hours as two different versions of the network led miners to unknowingly start building two separate chains (Andresen, 2013). The centralized leadership team quickly detected the split, and the miners on the more advanced node took a financial loss to downgrade and restore the canonical chain. An attack was made on a merchant during the accidental hard fork. After the incident, Bitcoin leadership released an upgrade to fix the problem and sent a series of alerts to users of older versions asking them to upgrade.

As the Bitcoin example illustrates, some early-stage FinTech projects could appear unstable in their infancy, but with time, they may grow into stable, valuable products or services. Safe harbors allow developers to gradually transition their product or service from centralized to decentralized control without being subject to costly compliance requirements. Safe harbors enable key figures in a startup's development, like founders, developers, and VCs, to monitor progress and respond quickly. However, an important consideration regulators need to make with any safe harbor or sunset provision is the definition or quantification of thresholds. Regulatory options typically include criteria like setting time limits or quantifying decentralization in terms of owners, miners, exchanges, and so on to grow out of or sunset your time in the safe harbor.

Many DeFi protocols are experimenting with transferring control to the user base through governance tokens and evaluating decentralization through voter engagement or other popular metrics for decentralization like Gini or Nakamoto coefficients (Srinivasan and Lee, 2017). Of course, when it comes to decentralization metrics, a natural question arises about how to weight accounts when users can have multiple accounts and some accounts are not active. But these are exactly the kind of questions that regulators, developers, and academics can collaborate on answering with real-world data after the fact (e.g., see work on re-centralization by Appel and Grennan (2023) and Cong et al. (2025)).

The size argument is a key advantage of safe harbors. Regulatory wait-and-see approaches are often justified because innovation in its infancy is too small to have a meaningful impact on financial stability. Safe harbors allow regulators to focus on FinTech applications that have scaled up to the point where they could impact the system. Fortunately, by providing a safe harbor, the regulators incentivize the developers and inventors to stay in the U.S. and engage with the current system rather than relocating to other jurisdictions.

In an insightful model of regulatory uncertainty, Campello et al. (2024) analyze FinTech development through a strategic game between innovative firms and a resource-constrained regulator. The framework captures how innovation rates depend on regulatory budgets, skills, and the number of competing innovators, with a key finding that multiple equilibria arise from the complementarity between regulatory preparedness and innovation investments. While the model's binary regulatory instruments (approve or ban) often capture the current crudeness of current FinTech regulation in the U.S., incorporating sunset provisions would address the multiplicity problem. Sunset provisions usually have time-limited approvals with renewal requirements. This could be a powerful equilibrium selection mechanism by creating a coordination device that anchors expectations and eliminates inefficient equilibria.

Taking the insights to the real world, it becomes clear that sunset provisions help formalize post-innovation learning, allowing regulators to allow innovators to enter the markets early and efficiently while preserving the option to terminate harmful innovations based on outcomes observed after the fact. While this has not been tried much with financial innovation, evidence from medical device regulation offers an intriguing parallel, as it shows post-market-entry surveillance meaningfully increases consumer surplus through reductions in consumer uncertainty (Grennan and Town, 2020). Approving FinTech products early but reviewing additional data after some time would encourage experimentation with potentially valuable innovations that might otherwise face outright bans.

By combining collaborative governance models like safe harbors and sandboxes with flexible legal frameworks such as sunset provisions, regulators could provide more concrete guidance for FinTech startups. In doing so, they could also achieve an adaptive regulatory system that better matches the new open-source, composable, customizable, easy-entrepreneurial entry financial ecosystem. In this spirit, regulators could even sunset their involvement in the regulatory system and allow RegTech tools or hybrid approaches to self-regulation to take over after a certain threshold of stability or maturity is achieved.

6 Conclusion

When banks introduced ATMs, they were not reinventing banking but increasing access by making it more convenient. The same goes for credit cards. These were iterations, not revolutions. These iterations typically involved incumbent financial service providers improving on existing core financial capabilities through singular product or process innovations. Yet something profoundly different is happening now. What we are witnessing today with FinTech innovation is not just another step or incremental innovation but a leap into an entirely new ecosystem. FinTech innovations, driven by advances in AI, blockchain, and their convergence (AI × crypto), are transforming financial services by building an entirely new financial infrastructure and expanding the core capabilities of the financial system itself.

I follow a temporal, three-act structure to analyze this profound transformation. In the past, financial innovation came from within (e.g., banks adding digital layers to analog processes). In the present, tech outsiders are creating parallel financial infrastructure that expands what money and assets can do, who or what can move them, and how they move. From an economic perspective, these innovations slash costs, simultaneously solving old economic inefficiencies yet introducing new ones. These changes make applications of existing legal precedent contentious (e.g., Howey Test), inapplicable (e.g., DEXs), or without legal analogy (AI × crypto). And in the future? Regulatory frameworks, designed for a world of physical branches and paper settlement, will need to adapt because traditional regulatory approaches do not match the players, infrastructure, and automated processes that underlie this new way of providing core financial capabilities.

What makes this moment unique is the simultaneous emergence of a rare confluence of transformative forces. First, AI's remarkable ability to reduce prediction and exploration costs is creating financial services that adapt to individual needs in real-time, such as having a semi-automated personal financial advisor who knows precisely when and how your circumstances change. Second, blockchain technology has accomplished something previously thought impossible: verifying state without centralized intermediaries. This creates trustless systems operating across borders with radical transparency (e.g., imagine financial transactions as visible and verifiable as passing an object from one hand to another, yet functioning globally). Third, and most significantly, the convergence of these technologies (AI × crypto) creates entirely new approaches to economic activity. Examples include agentic applications that autonomously manage digital assets and traditional resources to generate revenue as entrepreneurs, or new business entities that coordinate talent and development globally through smart-contract-based governance. These innovations represent more than the digitization of core financial capabilities, suggesting a need for regulation attuned to their complete capabilities.

The regulatory challenges these innovations present are also novel and fascinating. Traditional financial regulations evolved to address problems: information asymmetries between banks and customers, agency problems within hierarchical institutions, and systemic risks that could trigger economic collapse. This framework now faces fundamental questions: How does one regulate a DAO with no central authority? How does one assign liability when an AI agent, operating on a blockchain, makes autonomous financial decisions? How does one protect consumers in systems designed to eliminate intermediaries? These questions offer a glimpse into the perplexities regulators face when trying to find a regulatory solution that encourages innovation and entrepreneurial entry while continuing to safeguard capital formation and stability.

As my analyses demonstrate, these questions demand new rules and new ways of thinking about regulation. Adaptation is necessary. From a regulatory perspective, adaptation is more than mere policy updates. Instead, adaptation requires embracing RegTech solutions that leverage the technologies causing disruption, developing economic incentives that make compliance rational rather than merely mandatory, and fostering collaborative governance that brings diverse stakeholders to the table. In addition, adaptive regulation means taking proactive initiative by policing mischaracterizations before they mislead consumers, creating hybrid legal analogies for novel intersections like AI × crypto, and developing graduated frameworks recognizing varying degrees of risk rather than imposing binary classifications.

My investigation makes clear that the technologies creating regulatory challenges may offer solutions. Rather than merely confronting innovation as a threat, regulators could leverage technologies such as privacy-preserving regulatory oracles utilizing ZK-proofs to verify compliance without compromising confidentiality. It is also the case that effective oversight would benefit from embracing the inherent composability of FinTech innovations, allowing for tailored regulatory responses proportional to varying degrees of risk and decentralization. Addressing these complexities necessitates collaborative governance models involving regulators, technologists, academics, and consumer advocates. Such collaboration, however, must be carefully balanced against the threat of regulatory capture.

Safe harbor provisions offer one promising path forward, allowing developers to transition their projects through phases of decentralization without overwhelming compliance pressures during the fragile, early growth phases. Yet these safe harbors would best be tempered by sunset clauses that enable stakeholder-informed regulators to end experiments based on actual data rather than theoretical expectations. Similarly, aligning developer incentives with regulatory goals through mechanism design is promising as it can make compliance economically rational rather than merely mandatory. Proposals like cross-chain risk buffers and smart contract insurance pools exemplify this approach.

Finally, proactive definitional clarity will be essential. As legal frameworks evolve to encompass AI × crypto, regulators must carefully evaluate analogies drawn from corporate personhood, animal rights, and product liability to establish coherent and enforceable standards. Similarly, being proactive in enforcing against misrepresentation in data usage and decentralization claims is critical to uphold market transparency and trust.

In conclusion, evaluating FinTech innovation at a high level and through an economic and institutional lens reveals that regulating FinTech cannot simply follow previous solutions in the playbook, but, instead, an adaptive, proactive approach is best. While there is still a place for traditional solutions when the economic distortion is familiar, regulatory tools that better match the new financial infrastructure and emergent risks need to be adopted, such as RegTech and collaborative governance solutions. These more modern tools best harness the efficiency gains and benefits this wave of FinTech innovation brings while mitigating the new market failures and inefficiencies they produce. Promising areas for future research include empirical evaluations of regulatory adaptations, such as studies of the real effects of RegTech solutions, or theoretical models of optimal sunset thresholds.

References

Abadi, J., Brunnermeier, M., 2022. Blockchain economics. Working Paper.

Abis, S., 2020. Man vs. machine: Quantitative and discretionary equity management. Working Paper.

Adrian, T., Brunnermeier, M. K., 2016. Covar. American Economic Review 106, 1705–41.

Agrawal, A., Catalini, C., Goldfarb, A., 2014. Some simple economics of crowdfunding. Innovation Policy and the Economy 14, 63–97.

Agrawal, A., Gans, J., Goldfarb, A., 2018. Prediction Machines. Harvard Business Review Press, Boston, MA.

Agarwal, S., Lucca, D., Seru, A., Trebbi, F., 2014. Inconsistent regulators: Evidence from banking. Quarterly Journal of Economics 129, 889–938.

Akerlof, G. A., 1970. The market for "lemons": Quality uncertainty and the market mechanism. The Quarterly Journal of Economics 84, 488.

Andresen, G., 2013. March 2013 chain fork post-mortem. Comments.

Appel, I., Grennan, J., 2023. Control of decentralized autonomous organizations. AEA Papers and Proceedings 113, 182–185.

Appel, I., Grennan, J., 2024. Decentralized governance and digital asset prices. Working Paper.

Appel, I., Grennan, J., White, J., Wilkoff, S., 2025. Holding the bag: Depositor reactions to a crypto "shadow bank" collapse. Working Paper.

Aramonte, S., Huang, W., Schrimpf, A., 2021. DeFi risks and the decentralisation illusion. BIS Quarterly Review, December, 21–36.

Asker, J., Fershtman, C., Pakes, A., 2022. Artificial intelligence, algorithm design and pricing. AEA Papers and Proceedings.

Azar, P., Casillas, A., Farboodi, M., 2024. Information and market power in defi intermediation. Working Paper.

Balyuk, T., Williams, E., 2023. Friends and family money: P2P transfers and financially fragile consumers. Working Paper.

Bartlett, R., Morse, A., Stanton, R., Wallce, N., 2022. Consumer lending discrimination in the era of Fintech. Journal of Financial Economics, 143, 30–56.

Berg, T., Burg, V., Gombovic, A., Puri, M., 2020. On the rise of fintechs – credit scoring using digital footprints. Review of Financial Studies 33, 2845–289.

Berg, T., Burg, V., Keil, J., Puri, M., 2023. The economics of "buy now, paylater": A merchant's perspective. Working Paper.

Berle, A., Means, G., 1932. The Modern Corporation and Private Property. Taylor & Francis.

Bertsch, C., 2023. Adoption, fragility, and regulation of stablecoins. Working Paper.

Betley, J., Tan, D., Warncke, N., et al., 2025. Emergent misalignment: Narrow finetuning can produce broadly misaligned llms. Working Paper.

Bodó, B., Gervais, D., Quintais, J. P., 2018. Blockchain and smart contracts: The missing link in copyright licensing? International Journal of Law and Information Technology 26, 311–336.

Bongaerts, D., Lambert, T., Liebau, D., Roosenboom, P., 2025. Vote delegation in defi governance. Working Paper.

Borri, N., Liu, Y., Tsyvinski, A., 2022. The economics of non-fungible tokens. Working Paper.

Buchak, G., Matvos, G., Piskorski, T., Seru, A., 2018. Fintech, regulatory arbitrage, and the rise of shadow banks. Journal of Financial Economics 130, 453–483.

Budish, E., 2018. The economic limits of bitcoin and the blockchain. NBER Working Paper No. 24717.

Campello, M., Cong, L. W., Dietrich, D., 2024. Regulatory uncertainty and fintech innovation. Working Paper.

Cao, S., Jiang, W., Wang, J., Yang, B., 2022. From man vs. machine to man + machine: The art and AI of stock analyses. Working Paper.

Cao, S., Jiang, W., Yang, B., Zhang, A., 2020. How to talk when a machine is listening: Corporate disclosure in the age of AI. Working Paper.

Catalini, C., de Gortari, A., Shah, N., 2022. Some simple economics of stablecoins. Annual Review of Financial Economics 14, 117–135.

Catalini, C., Gans, J., 2020. Some simple economics of the blockchain. Communications of the ACM 63, 80–90.

Chang, J.-W., 2020. The economics of crowdfunding. American Economic Journal: Microeconomics 12, 257–280.

Chaparro, F., 2018. An activist crypto hedge fund launched today, and it's backed by digital currency group and peter thiel. The Block.

Citron, D. K., Wittes, B., 2017. The internet will not break: Denying bad samaritans section 230 immunity. Fordham Law Review.

Coglianese, C., Mendelson, E., 2010. Meta-regulation and self-regulation. The Oxford Handbook of Regulation pp. 145–168.

Cong, L. W., Feng, G., He, J., He, X., 2023a. Growing the efficient frontier on panel trees. NBER Working Paper No. 30805.

Cong, L. W., Grauer, K., Rabetti, D., Updegrave, H., 2023b. Blockchain forensics and crypto-related cybercrimes. Working Paper.

Cong, L. W., Harvey, C., Rabetti, D., Wu, Z.-Y., 2023c. An anatomy of crypto-enabled cybercrimes. Working Paper.

Cong, L. W., He, Z., 2019. Blockchain disruption and smart contracts. Review of Financial Studies 34, 1191–1235.

Cong, L. W., He, Z., Tang, K., 2023d. The tokenomics of staking. Working Paper.

Cong, L. W., Landsman, W., Maydew, E., Rabetti, D., 2023e. Tax-loss harvesting with cryptocurrencies. Journal of Accounting and Economics 76, 101607.

Cong, L. W., Li, X., Tang, K., Yang, Y., 2023f. Crypto wash trading. Management Science.

Cong, L. W., Mayer, S., 2022. Antitrust and user union in the era of digital platforms and big data. Working Paper 69, 6427–6454.

Cong, L. W., Rabetti, D., Yan, Y., Wang, C., 2025. Centralized governance in decentralized organizations. Working Paper.

Cong, L. W., Tang, K., Wang, J., Zhang, Y., 2021. Alphaportfolio: Direct construction through reinforcement learning and interpretable ai. Working Paper.

Cong, L. W., Tang, K., Wang, J., Zhang, Y., 2022. Deep sequence modeling: Development and applications in asset pricing. Journal of Financial Data Science 3, 28–42.

Cong, L. W., Tang, K., Wang, Y., Zhao, X., 2023g. Inclusion and democratization through web3 and defi? Initial evidence from the ethereum ecosystem. Working Paper 30949, National Bureau of Economic Research.

Cong, L. W., Xiao, Y., 2021. Categories and Functions of Crypto-Tokens. IN M. Pompella, & R. Matousek (eds.). Handbook of FinTech and Blockchain, Palgrave MacMillan.

D'Acunto, F., Prabhala, N., Rossi, A. G., 2019. The promises and pitfalls of robo-advising. Review of Financial Studies 32, 1983–2020.

Dambra, M., Field, L. C., Gustafson, M. T., 2015. The jobs act and ipo volume: Evidence that disclosure costs affect the ipo decision. Journal of Financial Economics 116, 121–143.

Dessaint, O., Foucault, T., Fresard, L., 2024. Does alternative data improve financial forecasting? the horizon effect. The Journal of Finance 79, 2237–2287.

Egan, M., Matvos, G., Seru, A., 2019. The market for financial adviser misconduct. Journal of Political Economy 127, 233–295.

Eldar, O., Grennan, J., 2023. Common venture capital investors and startup growth. The Review of Financial Studies 37, 549–590.

Ferrer, E. C., Berman, I., Kapitonov, A., Manaenko, V., Chernyaev, M., Tarasov, P., 2023. Gaka-chu: A self-employed autonomous robot artist. In: *2023 IEEE*

International Conference on Robotics and Automation (ICRA), IEEE, pp. 11583–11589.

Foldy, B., Ostroff, C., 2024. How a colorful investor profited from a crypto giant's dealmaking. Wall Street Journal.

Foley, S., Karlsen, J. R., Putniņš, T. J., 2019. Sex, Drugs, and Bitcoin: How Much Illegal Activity Is Financed through Cryptocurrencies? Review of Financial Studies 32, 1798–1853.

Foreman, M., Grennan, J., Marian, M., Menzer, T., 2023. Common sense recommendations for the application of tax law to digital assets. Joint Committee on Taxation Comment Letter.

Frankfurter, F., 1939. Nardone v. United States. Cornell Law School Legal Information Institute Cornell Law School Legal Information Institute.

Freixas, X., Rochet, J.-C., 2008. Microeconomics of Banking. MIT Press: Cambridge, MA.

Friedman, J. N., Holden, R. T., 2008. Optimal gerrymandering: Sometimes pack, but never crack. American Economic Review 98, 113–144.

Gans, J. S., Holden, R., 2022. A solomonic solution to ownership disputes: An application to blockchain front-running. Working Paper.

Gertler, P., Higgins, S., Malmendier, U., Ojeda, W., 2025. Do behavioral frictions prevent firms from adopting profitable opportunities? Working Paper 33387, National Bureau of Economic Research.

Goldfarb, A., Tucker, C., 2012. Shifts in privacy concerns. American Economic Review 102, 349–353.

Goldfarb, A., Tucker, C., 2019. Digital economics. Journal of Economic Literature., 47, 3–43.

Gompers, P., Ishii, J., Metrick, A., 2003. Corporate governance and equity prices. The Quarterly Journal of Economics 118, 107–156.

Gorton, G. B., Zhang, J., 2021. Taming wildcat stablecoins. Working Paper.

Graham, J. R., Grennan, J., Harvey, C. R., Rajgopal, S., 2022. Corporate culture: Evidence from the field. Journal of Financial Economics 146, 552–593.

Grennan, J., 2025. Cryptocurrency regulation: Protective vs. enabling approaches. Working Paper.

Grennan, J., Liu, Z.-X., Tan, J., 2025. A lottery approach to memecoins. Working Paper.

Grennan, J., Michaely, R., 2021. FinTechs and the market for financial analysis. Journal of Financial and Quantitative Analysis 56, 1877–1907.

Grennan, J., Michaely, R., 2022. Artificial intelligence and high-skilled work: Evidence from analysts. Working Paper.

Grennan, J., Michaely, R., 2025. The deleveraging of U.S. firms and the role of institutional investors. Working Paper.

Grennan, M., Town, R. J., 2020. Regulating innovation with uncertain quality: Information, risk, and access in medical devices. American Economic Review 110, 120–61.

Griffin, J. M., 2021. Ten years of evidence: Was fraud a force in the financial crisis? Journal of Economic Literature 59, 1293–1321.

Grossman, G. M., Helpman, E., 2002. Special Interest Politics. MIT Press.

Gupta, A., Nishesh, N., Simintzi, E., 2024. Big data and bigger firms: A labor market channel. Working Paper.

Hall, B. H., 2009. Business and financial method patents, innovation, and policy. Scottish Journal of Political Economy 56, 443–473.

Hart, O., Landemore, H., Zingales, L., 2024. How to implement shareholder democracy. George J. Stigler Center Working Paper No. 350.

Harvey, C., Ramachandran, A., Santoro, J., 2021. DeFi and the Future of Finance. Wiley.

Harvey, C. R., Hasbrouck, J., Saleh, F., 2024. The evolution of decentralized exchange: Risks, benefits, and oversight. Working Paper.

Hellmann, T., Puri, M., 2002. Venture capital and the professionalization of start-up firms: Empirical evidence. The Journal of Finance 57, 169–197.

Holden, R., Malani, A., 2021. Can blockchain solve the hold-up problem in contracts? Elements in Law, Economics and Politics Cambridge University Press.

Holden, R., Malani, A., 2022. The law and economics of blockchain. Annual Review of Law and Social Science 18, 297–313.

Howell, S. T., Niessner, M., Yermack, D., 2020. Initial coin offerings; financing groth with cryptocurreny token sales. Review of Financial Studies 33, 3925–3974.

Huang, D., Goetzmann, W., 2023. Selection-neglect in the NFT bubble. NBER Working Paper No. 31498.

John, K., Monnot, B., Mueller, P., Saleh, F., Schwarz-Schilling, C., 2024. Economics of ethereum. Working Paper.

John, K., O'Hara, M., Saleh, F., 2022. Bitcoin and beyond. Annual Review of Financial Economics 14, 95–115.

John, K., Rivera, T., Saleh, F., 2025. Proof-of-work versus proof-of-stake: A comparative economic analysis. Review of Financial Studies 38, 1955–2004.

Judge, K., 2015. Intermediary influence. University of Chicago Law Review 82, 573.

Kahneman, D., 2013. Thinking, Fast and Slow. Farrarm Straus and Giroux.

Kappos, D. J., Bennett, D. S., Mariani, M. E., et al., 2023. Nfts, incentives and control: Tecnical mechanisms and intellectual property rights. Stanford Journal of Blockchain Law and Policy 6, 93–118.

Kharif, O., 2025. Trump Is in Crypto's Corner. The Public's Trust Is Not.

Lambert, T., Liebau, D., Roosenboom, P., 2021. Secruity token offerings. Small Business Economics 59(1), 299–325.

Lee, J., Li, T., Shin, D., 2021. The wisdom of crowds in fintech: Evidence from initial coin offerings. Review of Corporate Finance Studies 11, 1–46.

Lehar, A., Parlour, C., 2024. Decentralized exchanges. Working Paper.

Lerner, J., Seru, A., Short, N., Sun, Y., 2024. Financial innovation in the twenty-first century: Evidence from us patents. Journal of Political Economy 132, 1391–1449.

Lerner, J., Tufano, P., 2012. The Rate and Direction of Inventive Activity Revisited, University of Chicago Press, chap. The Consequences of Financial Innovation: A Counterfactual Research Agenda.

Li, T., Shin, D., Wang, B., 2021. Cryptocurrency pump-and-dump schemes. Working Paper.

Liu, J., Makarov, I., Schoar, A., 2023. Anatomy of a run: The terra luna crash. NBER Working Paper No.31160

Loo, R. V., 2021. Federal rules of platform procedure. University of Chicago Law Review 88, 829.

Lyandres, E., Palazzo, B., Rabetti, D., 2022. Initial coin offering (ico) success and post-ico performance. Management Science 68, 8658–8679.

Lyandres, E., Rabetti, D., 2023. Initial Coin Offerings, Springer, pp. 1–6.

Maggio, M. D., Katz, J., Williams, E., 2023. Buy now, pay later credit: User characteristics andeffects on spending patterns. Working Paper.

Malinova, K., Park, A., 2023. Tokenomics: When tokens beat equity. Management Science 69, 6568–6583.

Manne, H. G., 1965. Mergers and the market for corporate control. Journal of Political Economy 73, 110–120.

Mattli, W., Woods, N., 2009. In Whose Benefit? Explaining Regulatory Change in Global Politics, Princeton University Press, pp. 1–43.

McCurdy, W., 2024. Stripe inks $1.1 billion deal to buy stablecoin platform bridge. Decrypt.

Meling, T., Mostad, M., Vestre, A., 2024. Crypto tax evasion. NBER Working Paper No. 32865.

Mishra, P., Prabhala, N., Rajan, R. G., 2022. The relationship dilemma: Why do banks differ in the pace at which they adopt new technology? The Review of Financial Studies 35, 3418–3466.

Nakamoto, S., 2008. Bitcoin: A peer-to-peer electronic cash system. www.bitcoin.org.

Ogus, A., 1995. Rethinking self-regulation. Oxford Journal of Legal Studies 15, 97–108.

Oh, S., Rosen, S., Zhang, A. L., 2024. Digital veblen goods. Working Paper.

Ohlhaver, P., Weyl, E. G., Buterin, V., 2022. Decentralized society: Finding web3's soul. Working Paper.

Partz, H., 2025. House Democrats propose bill to ban presidential memecoins: Report.

Philippon, T., 2016. The fintech opportunity. Working Paper 22476, National Bureau of Economic Research.

Saleh, F., 2020. Blockchain without waste: Proof-of-stake. Review of Financial Studies 34, 1156–1190.

Schar, F., 2021. Decentralized finance: On blockchain- and smart contract-basedfinancial markets. Federal Reserve Bank of St. Louis Review, 103 (2), 153–174.

Schumpeter, J. A., 1934. The theory of economic development: An inquiry into profits, capital, credit, interest, and the business cycle Cambridge: Harvard University Press.

SEC, 2022. Amendments to exchange act rule 3b-16 regarding the definition of exchange.

SEC, 2025. Staff Statement on Meme Coins.

Smith, M. D., Alstyne, M. V., 2021. It's time to update section 230. Harvard Business Review.

Sockin, M., Xiong, W., 2022. Decentralization through tokenization. Journal of Finance.

Srinivasan, B. S., Lee, L., 2017. Quantifying decentralization 78, 247–299. https://news.earn.com/quantifying-decentralization-e39db233c28e.

Stigler, G. J., 1971. The theory of economic regulation. Bell Journal of Economics and Management Science 2, 3.

Strausz, R., 2017. A theory of crowdfunding: A mechanism design approach with demand uncertainty and moral hazard. American Economic Review 107, 1430–1476.

Tan, J., Grennan, J., Devjani, H., Schmid, B., Boothroyd, F., 2025. State of dao m&a. DAOstar Research Series.

Tang, V. W., Zhang, T. Q., 2021. Regulation, tax, and cryptocurrency pricing. Working Paper.

Tufano, P., 2003. Financial Innovation, Elsevier, 1 (Part A) 307–335.

Weyl, E. G., Thorburn, L., de Keulenaar, E., Mcchangama, J., Siddarth, D., Tang, A., 2025. Prosocial media. Working Paper.

White, J. T., Wilkoff, S., Yildiz, S., 2022. The role of the media in speculative markets: Evidence from non-fungible tokens (nfts). Working Paper

Yaffe-Bellany, D., Griffith, E., Schleifer, T., 2024. How crypto money is poised to influence the election. New York Times June 17.

Yermack, D., 2017. Corporate Governance and Blockchains. Review of Finance 21, 7–31.

Yiu, S., Seamans, R., Raj, M., Liu, T., 2024. Strategic responses to technological change: Evidence from chatgpt and upwork. Working Paper.

YouGov, 2024. Cryptoassets consumer research 2024. Wave 5 Report on Behalf of the Financial Conduct Authority.

Acknowledgments

I thank Avi Goldfarb, Lubomir Litov, Daniel Rock, Raghu Rau, Josh Tan, Rory Van Loo, and seminar participants at the OCC Symposium on the Implications of Financial Technology for Banking and Berkeley (Haas) for helpful comments on an earlier draft of this study. I am grateful to the Lab for Inclusive FinTech (LIFT) for funding to support this research. I thank Adrienne Davis and Samantha Henze for their excellent research assistance. Any remaining errors are my own.

Cambridge Elements

Law, Economics and Politics

Series Editor in Chief
Carmine Guerriero, *University of Bologna*

Series Co-Editors
Alessandro Riboni, *École Polytechnique*
Jillian Grennan, *Emory University*
Petros Sekeris, *TBS Education*

Series Managing Editor
Valentino Moscariello, *University of Bologna*

Series Associate Editors
Maija Halonen-Akatwijuka, *University of Bristol*
Sara Biancini, *Université de Cergy-Pontoise*
Melanie Meng Xue, *London School of Economics and Political Science*
Claire Lim, *Queen Mary University of London*
Andy Hanssen, *Clemson University*
Giacomo Benati, *Eberhard Karls University, Tübingen*

About the Series

Decisions taken by individuals are influenced by formal and informal institutions. Legal and political institutions determine the nature, scope and operation of markets, organisations and states. This interdisciplinary series analyses the functioning, determinants, and impact of these institutions, organizing the existing knowledge and guiding future research.

Cambridge Elements ≡

Law, Economics and Politics

Elements in the Series

The Strategic Analysis of Judicial Behavior: A Comparative Perspective
Lee Epstein and Keren Weinshall

Can Blockchain Solve the Hold-up Problem in Contracts?
Richard Holden and Anup Malani

Deep IV in Law
Zhe Huang, Xinyue Zhang, Ruofan Wang and Daniel L. Chen

Reform for Sale: A Common Agency Model with Moral Hazard Frictions
Perrin Lefebvre and David Martimort

A Safety Valve Model of Equity as Anti-opportunism
Kenneth Ayotte, Ezra Friedman and Henry E. Smith

More is Less: Why Parties May Deliberately Write Incomplete Contracts
Maija Halonen-Akatwijuka and Oliver Hart

Corruption and the Voter's Decision: Experimental Evidence from Brazil
Miguel F. P. de Figueiredo

U.S. Innovation Inequality and Trumpism
Victor Menaldo, Nicolas Wittstock

FinTech Regulation in the United States: Past, Present, and Future
Jillian Grennan

A full series listing is available at: www.cambridge.org/ELEP